MARKET
CHRONICLES

STORIES & RECIPES FROM MONTREAL'S

Marché Jean-Talon

Semenak, Susan
Market Chronicles
Stories & Recipes from Montreal's Marché Jean-Talon

ISBN : 978-2-920943-85-8

Photography: Albert Elbilia ... elbilia.com
Historical photographs: Les Archives de la Ville de Montréal (p. 24 & 26)
Design and production director: Albert Elbilia ... elbilia.com
Illustrations: Susan Semenak
Graphic designer: Stéphane Losq
Copy editor: Sheila Scott

Executive editor: Antoine Trempe
First assistant: Sara Dufour

The publisher acknowledges the financial support of the Government of Canada through the Canada Book Fund (CBF) for its publishing activities and the support of the Government of Quebec through the tax credit for book publishing program (SODEC).

Legal Deposit: 2011
Bibliothèque et Archives du Québec
Library and Archives Canada

Printed in Canada by Friesens

to Daniel, my *soulmate.*

MARKET CHRONICLES

STORIES & RECIPES FROM MONTREAL'S
Marché Jean-Talon

SUSAN SEMENAK

FOREWORD BY ÉRIC DUPUIS
PHOTOGRAPHY BY ALBERT ELBILIA

cardinal

FOREWORD

by Éric Dupuis

Executive Chef, Dominion Square Tavern, Montreal

"Off to the market!"

It's a universal rallying call. In Quebec, Jean Talon Market is my favourite place to shop, no matter the season. Summer or winter, the market is abuzz with activity. Day and night, its hard-working producers and devoted vendors bring in the fruits of their labours. There is an incredible variety of foods offered here, locally grown or from far-off lands.

Some of these people have been at the market since the 1960s, others only since last summer. All of them are happy and proud to let us glimpse their everyday lives. Fruits and vegetables, meat and poultry, fish and seafood, cheese, spices, potted plants, even Christmas trees — these are some of the things professional chefs as well as home cooks buy at Marché Jean-Talon.

The market is a rich source of inspiration for everyone, but especially for people in the food industry, who need constant renewal. As an executive chef, I can't help listening in on conversations at the market. I love talking with the vendors, sharing trials and tribulations, and the joys of our everyday lives. It's a way of feeling connected with them and with the earth; the long-reaching roots of these farmers span generations.

Jean Talon Market will truly inspire you on many levels. Meeting the people at the market and getting to know them is sure to whet your appetite.

These recipes will enrich your family dinners. This book will make you want to head for Jean Talon Market and make it your own.

Happy reading!

•CoNTeNTS•

La Vallée-du
Bleu

2.⁰⁰

Tomate
Sapori
du
Québec
$ 3.⁰⁰ ch.
each.

2 pour
For $ 5.⁰⁰

- JEAN TALON MARKET -

(A love story)

Every inch of table and countertop in my kitchen is taken up with bags and boxes spilling over with leaves, roots and fruits. A colander of hot peppers for roasting sits next to a tub of rumpled Swiss chard. Minestrone soup bubbles on the stove and a plum cake rises in the oven, dulling the early fall chill and infusing the house with the smell of cinnamon and brown sugar. Still, there is hardly a dent in the mountains of food hauled home from Jean Talon Market this morning. For dinner tonight: a pork shoulder to slow-roast with garlic, rosemary and Cortland apples from the Gingras family orchard. On the side, we'll have mashed potatoes — heirloom Rattes with a nutty flavour and buttery texture from Daniel Oligny's farm in St-Rémi. And sautéed torpedo shallots — Jacques Rémillard handed them over the counter with a mischievous look; their rocket shape is such an oddity.

It is impossible to resist the market's charms, especially at harvest time. From June to October, when the stalls are flush with fresh, local produce, there is no more sensual place in all of Montreal than Marché Jean-Talon, the sprawling labyrinth of farmers' stands, butcher stalls, bakeries, spice shops and fish stores tucked in among Little Italy's espresso bars and triplexes. Boisterous and unbound, it is to Montreal what La Boqueria is to Barcelona, what the Mercato di Rialto is to Venice and Union Square Greenmarket to New York. It is a window on a city that loves to eat, a sample of who we are and how we live. From spring through fall, the market makes room for nearly 150 vendors over nearly 220,000 square feet. It is the largest open-air farmers' market in North America and a showcase for Quebec's bounty of fruits and vegetables, its prize-winning cheeses and meats, and the crab, lobster and shrimp fished from its Gulf of St. Lawrence shores. No chain stores or fast-food franchises, no T-shirt vendors or souvenir stands, our favourite market is all about food. On weekend mornings Jean Talon Market is a crush of people strolling the aisles, pushing strollers and pulling wagons, toddlers wedged between cauliflower heads or strawberry crates.

The first thing you want to do upon arriving is eat. Everybody, it seems, is noshing from grease-spotted bags and layered napkins: corn on the cob, churros, Belgian-style frites. Fried squid, buffalo brochettes, baguettes stuffed with merguez sausage and spicy harissa, jam-filled Polish doughnuts. We brush away the crumbs after the last bite of maple tartelette, then succumb to free samples of jambon cru and watermelon. This is the place to shop for the week's provisions — potatoes, carrots, apples, bread, a chicken for soup — but also to experiment with new varieties and unusual hybrids. The fruits, vegetables, meats and cheeses here come with whimsical names and in a panoply of unexpected colours, shapes and sizes. Meet a curly-leaf lettuce called Lola and a voluptuous strawberry named Jewel. How about a conical cheese called Le Sein d'Hélène (Helen's breast) or L'Hercule de Charlevoix, a robust cheese named after a local strongman?

Even in winter, when the market shrinks back and retreats indoors, Marché Jean-Talon is Montreal's gastronomic soul. At the Brûlerie aux Quatre Vents, its roasted-coffee aromas filling the market halls, patrons huddle reading the paper, avoiding the bluster outside. The butchers stock venison, boar, rabbit and lamb from Kamouraska. Down the aisle, the cheesemonger at Qui Lait Cru wraps up a wheel of Riopelle de l'Isle, a hunk of Louis d'Or and a wedge of Bleu Bénédictin – a cheese platter with an impressive pedigree. Every single selection is an award-winning artisanal Quebec cheese.

Whatever the season, Jean Talon Market is a place where urban and rural meet, where city dwellers come to buy food from the farmers who grew it, reconnecting with the land along the way. The signs above the farmers' stalls read like a genealogy of rural Quebec: Tremblay, Trottier, Lauzon and Palardy. Old-stock, *vieille souche* farming families are the descendants of New France habitants who cleared and cultivated these fertile St. Lawrence River Valley fields more than 300 years ago. They are joined by a new generation of organic growers and artisanal food crafters. To add to the mix, the owners of the more recent indoor shops are a cosmopolitan crew of spice-sellers, pasta-makers, pastry chefs and charcutiers. Marché Jean-Talon is a microcosm of Montreal: a francophone metropolis that speaks a hundred other languages, where here and there cultures collide in a smoked-meat pizza or a spring roll stuffed with rice noodles and *rosbif*. Where a jar of homemade pickled vegetables might be chutney, salsa, ketchup or kimchee.

Ever since the market's beginnings in the early 1930s, waves of immigrants to Montreal from Italy, Ireland, Poland and Ukraine, then Portugal and Greece, Morocco and Tunisia, El Salvador, Vietnam, Mexico, Lebanon and Haiti — and countless points in between — have come here to find inexpensive fruits and vegetables. This is where the city's Italians come for their carloads of plum tomatoes when it is time to "make the sauce" and where Muslims from Tunisia, Algeria and Morocco gravitate on Ramadan evenings in search of sweet, sticky chebakia to break the fast. Mexicans hankering for authentic *barbacoa* follow their noses to Javier Muñoz's *taqueria* on Saturday mornings, when the smell of spiced lamb barbecued in clay-lined pits fills the air. Around the market's perimeter, Italian bakers and grocers, Latino butchers, and hole-in-the-wall tonkinoise soup and shish taouk joints lend their world beat to the vibe.

But it is what's for sale inside the market proper, at the farmers' stands and meat and cheese stalls, that makes Montrealers proudest of all. There is a food revolution afoot in Quebec, as elsewhere, and the province's chefs, home cooks and environmentalists are embracing local, regional and artisanal food. "Short circuits" is the new buzzword for sustainable food chains. It is the phrase local-food advocates use when they campaign for better access to food grown, raised or produced on family farms and in small-scale operations close to where it will be eaten. There is a growing awareness of the environmental and social costs of importing food over long distances and of the value of supporting local farmers. But there is more to it than lofty principles.

Taking home leafy carrots in a string-tied bouquet and grass-fed beef that never touched a Styrofoam tray brings its own soulful pleasure. The market's shoppers come for various reasons. To start, the prices are competitive and the food is always fresh. At the height of the growing season, new stock arrives at the market in the middle of the night and throughout the day, unloaded by bleary-eyed farmers who will take a nap in their trucks before heading back to the farm, leaving behind a crew of spouses, children, in-laws and hired help to man their stalls. "If you just love food, it will be about better taste. If you are worried about food safety, you will be looking for traceability. If you are really into the environment, you'll care about the smaller footprint," says Nancy Hinton, a chef and local-food proponent. "For me, it's about all those things and also about community. About supporting the people around me who work hard and care about what they do and take care of nature."

Just how local can you go in a big city like Montreal, set in a harsh northern climate? Thanks to technological advances in planting, hydroponic growing and produce refrigeration, eating local all year long isn't only possible, it's easy. Compared with most other North American cities, where urban sprawl has pushed agriculture farther and farther away, Montreal is blessed with adjacent farmland. After a day's work, many of Jean Talon Market's vendors can be back home on the farm in 45 minutes, barring traffic. Indeed, 80 per cent of Quebec's growers are within 60 kilometres of Montreal in places like St-Rémi, Ste-Clotilde and St-Eustache — even as close as neighbouring Laval, with its encroaching subdivisions. It's a pretty short circuit, for instance, when Daniel Racine loads up the van with strawberries picked from his fields in Ste-Anne-des-Plaines early in the morning, drives a half-hour to his stand at the market and unloads them in time for his customers to buy them, take them home and bake them into a strawberry pie for dessert that evening. It helps that Montreal sits in the St. Lawrence River Valley, surrounded by some of the most fertile soil in all of northeastern North America, with a microclimate conducive to growing fruits and vegetables.

For a long time, half of Quebec's harvest was grown by megaproducers and destined for export. Recently, the picture has begun to include a small but determined number of small-scale producers who have dispensed with distributors. Jean Talon Market's proximity and its relatively low stall-holder rental fees mean these small producers can sell directly to their customers, without bar codes or middlemen. The wide variety of their offerings and their willingness to grow new (and old, heirloom) varieties promotes biodiversity and is key to a sustainable food supply, says Isabelle St-Germain, a food activist with Equiterre, a Montreal-based organization that promotes food security and sustainability.

Some, like the potato grower Daniel Oligny and vegetable farmers Liette and Jean-Claude Lauzon, downsized and turned to the market after decades of selling to wholesalers. It was their way of wresting back control of their lives and their labours. Oligny still remembers the warehouse full of rotting cabbages he was stuck with after the terrorist attacks on New York City in 2001, when his U.S. customers stopped calling. Now he grows only what he can sell at the market or at a handful of grocery stores near his farm on Montreal's South Shore. The Lauzons used to farm 250 acres in St-Eustache, selling most of their produce to distributors. It ended up in restaurants and supermarkets up and down the east coast. When the pace grew too hectic and price fluctuations too nerve-racking, they sold some of their land and regrouped. Now they cultivate 70-some acres and almost everything they grow winds up in a mesh bag or bushel basket at Jean Talon Market. Chances are it will be Liette herself who bags it and hands it over. "I like knowing the people who eat the food I grew. I know them and they know me," she says, transferring Cortland apples from a giant wooden crate to smaller baskets. "And they like my stories from the farm and my recipes and secrets for cooking Brussels sprouts or choosing watermelon. These are not the kind of interactions you have at the supermarket."

For a clientele of food lovers fed up with the fluorescent-lit sterility of big-box stores and the static stroll down the supermarket aisle – where you can buy everything under the sun but nothing ever changes – the market is a kaleidoscope. Nothing is the same here two days in a row, the offerings coming and going with the unfolding of the seasons and the vagaries of the weather. You don't need a calendar to know it's spring; at the first whiff of thaw, there is maple syrup for sale and the Birri brothers, Lino and Bruno, haul out sacks of topsoil and compost for eager city gardeners. Two weeks of unexpected heat in April and the fiddleheads are in, disappearing as quickly as they arrived when the temperature plunges again.

Fat, juicy strawberries that stain your hands mean summer is here, while the crisp crunch of an Empire apple means that it is over.

- MARKET HISTORY -

(Est. Montreal - 1933)

Unlike most civic landmarks, Jean Talon Market doesn't boast imposing archways or a grand entrance. Instead, to get to the farmers' stalls, shoppers must jostle with cars and delivery vans on the rutted streets flanking the market to the north and south. It has come to be a tourist destination and a Montreal treasure, but at heart Marché Jean-Talon belongs to Little Italy. Laundry hangs on clotheslines and roses ramble up the backyard fences along Henri Julien Ave. Every now and then, someone will holler from the balcony of his duplex, fist waving at a beeping forklift as it backs up with a pre-dawn load of cabbage. But mostly the market and its neighbours exist in symbiotic harmony.

Jean Talon Market opened in 1933 as Le Marché du Nord in an expanding immigrant neighbourhood in the city's north end. Then as now, it sat just south of busy, commercial Jean Talon St. (named after the first intendant of New France) and a block east of St. Laurent Blvd., with its tramway line. On Fridays and Saturdays, growers from nearby farms drove up in their trucks and hauled out their bushels and crates, staying all day — or until the stock sold out. Before long Jean Talon Market was spilling out of its formal digs. Butcher shops and bakeries opened in bungalows and converted garages on the market's periphery.

The site had long been a lacrosse field, the Shamrock Lacrosse Grounds. In the aftermath of the stock market crash of 1929, the city of Montreal bought the field and the clubhouse and set about building a public market — part of a public works program aimed at creating jobs. The market's centrepiece would be a new yellow-brick Art Deco building with cornice motifs and an exterior wall clock. Soon enought long, open cement canopies were added to offer outdoor vendors protection from the elements.

Growers sold the limited variety of produce they had: beans, tomatoes, cucumbers, berries and lettuce in summer; apples in the fall; and root vegetables, squash and cabbage to store for winter. And while nobody knows how to pluck a chicken or skin a rabbit anymore, for decades people came to Jean Talon Market to buy their poultry and meat, alive and clucking or bleating. On hot summer days the smell from the stalls belonging to the chicken, pigeon and goat sellers and rabbit breeders was almost unbearable. Shoppers would take home their Sunday-dinner chickens in burlap sacks, the birds' legs tied to keep them from escaping, though it sometimes happened that one would get loose on the bus ride home.

This was a propitious site for a market, wedged as it was between fertile farmlands to the north in Laval and Mascouche and the growing population of Little Italy, a clientele eager for fresh, inexpensive food. The district was home to francophones,

Poles and Portuguese. But it was the scores of Italian immigrants who moved here in the early 1900s who made it their own. They had been enticed by the affordable lots and jobs in nearby greystone quarries, expanding railways and factories. They built modest houses and planted rambling vegetable gardens in their backyards. What they didn't eat themselves they sold across the fence to their neighbours or the market's customers.

Elena Faita's kitchen store, Quincaillerie Dante, and her cooking school, Mezza Luna, are Little Italy institutions. Her mother, Teresa Masecchia, like many Italians in the neighbourhood, worked at *il mercato* – across the street from the second-storey flat where the family lived. What do Italians eat, the farmer she worked for would ask? Soon he began growing eggplant, hot peppers and radicchio, and Teresa was teaching the customers how to make pesto and pasta sauce. Before long, Jean Talon Market had taken on a decidedly Italian flavour.

By the late 1960s, many of Montreal's markets began to disappear as the age of convenience food and spanking-new supermarkets took hold. Concerns over hygiene and food safety spurred city officials to prohibit the sale of livestock. Jean Talon Market faded as the number of customers dwindled and farmers stopped coming. Eventually, though, farmers' markets were back in vogue. By 2000, Jean Talon Market was bursting at its seams: weekend traffic jams were a nightmare and all summer long there was no place to park.

A plan for expansion in 2004 included underground parking, a new row of outdoor stalls and a wing of indoor boutiques to add life to the market year round. Urban planners toured famous, world-class markets for inspiration. They took their cue from Pike Place Market in Seattle, Granville Island market in Vancouver, and Paris's colourful Marché de la rue Mouffetard, where merchants roll out their counters every morning, bringing market life right into the street. In their search for new tenants, market officials looked to capitalize on the growing appetite for local, artisanal products and a burgeoning culture of foodies who seek out handmade pasta, local sheep's-milk cheese and organic olive oil. The changes didn't come without a fight, though. The market's very soul was in jeopardy, neighbours protested and old-time vendors grumbled about the newcomers. Now, it is as if they have always been there.

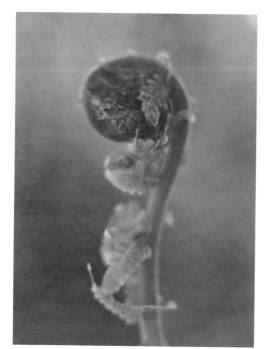

– SPRING –

(Seed)

....

Shoppers and vendors have roused themselves from their winter hibernation and arrived, as if on cue. Spring sneaks in at the market on the first warm weekend of March. François Brouillard has foraged day lily shoots from the soggy riverbank behind his house an hour northeast of Montreal. His wild edibles, laid out like bouquets on an otherwise bare table, are the first local colour and crunch we've had in months. The butcher at the corner is outside grilling sausage — bison, venison, veal and tofu. Winter-weary shoppers wander with bags of salty, fresh-fried potato chips or spicy onion bhajis, tilting their faces toward the sun. On these first days of spring, when the sun actually holds heat, no one is hunched and hurried anymore.

Early spring's best-loved heroes are the maple syrup vendors in their kitschy barnboard shacks. The new harvest of syrup is just in, and it is sweet-tooth heaven here: stretchy maple taffy, crumbly maple sugar, whipped and frothy maple butter and miniature taffy-filled cones. Everything, it seems, is *à l'érable* – ice cream, brandy, pork sausages and brioche.

At the end of April, workers take down the market's winter carapace. By May Day, the walls are gone and the breeze billows in as the market sprawls out to full size. The farmers turn up with their earliest offerings, meagre compared with what is to come. The danger of overnight frost prevents them from planting most of their crops until the middle of May. Even then there will be sleepless nights fretting over sudden thermometer dips.

But what's here is special — green and tender, local food that didn't travel a thousand kilometres. Mylène Dupont has brought pencil-thin spring leeks she planted last fall. She has pots of pansies and lettuces from her greenhouses, and baby white turnips, too. Many farmers whose fields are still bare are selling imported pineapples, mangoes and grapefruits. Others who refuse to sell anything they didn't grow themselves won't set up until later in the season. Soon pink nordic shrimp will arrive from Sept-Îles, and snow crab fished from Gaspé's northern shores as soon as the ice melts. Then asparagus, radishes and lettuce, impervious to the spring chill.

By the end of May, Jean Talon Market is in high gear. Gardening season sees the asphalt transformed into a field of vegetable seedlings and flower flats. The city's backyard and balcony gardeners are pouring in, on bikes and skateboards, in minivans. They haul home more tomato plants and geranium pots than they know what to do with.

Spring at last!!! The first signs of green make our hearts skip a beat.

029

· THE SPRING-CATCHERS ·

René Lussier & France Bisson

Spring arrives in St-Damase not as a date on the calendar but with the ping, pling, ping of sap dripping into galvanized buckets. In early March, when the weather offers the magical mix of below-freezing nights and warm days, maple sap begins to flow. René Lussier and his wife, France Bisson, hang a few old-fashioned buckets to capture the first sounds of spring, but these days their maple grove is laced with a web of plastic tubing. Clear, watery sap from tiny holes drilled into the trunks of their silver maples collects and flows fast through the tubing, gushing into a giant reservoir down the hill.

Outside the sky is blue and hopeful and the forest floor is a deep, brown soup of mud and melting snow. Inside the sugar shack the air is warm and thick with steam, wood smoke and the caramel smell of sap simmering down into sweet, golden maple syrup. The darkness is pierced by slivers of daylight sneaking in through barnboard cracks and the orange glow from the firebox when the Lussiers' son Dominique throws in another log. Up and down the dirt road, the neighbours are sugaring off too, and plumes of smoke and steam billow from the rusty rooftops.

The Lussiers' *cabane à sucre*, in the shadow of Mont St. Hilaire just east of Montreal, has years of Québécois tradition behind it. For generations, men headed into the woods at the first sign of spring, to rickety little sheds where they boiled sap and drank *caribou de cabane*, a sweet and potent blend of hot maple reduction and liquor. On weekends, the whole family would gather there, bringing beans, bread and ham and the makings for a feast. Forty years ago, René's father, Jean-Claude, bought an abandoned train station in the village, hoisted it onto wooden skids and dragged it with a bulldozer over three kilometres of frozen fields. It sat idle for nearly a decade while they saved the money to restore the building and outfit it for maple sugaring. Now the Lussiers produce more than 1,000 gallons a year.

"There's a special pride and joy that Quebecers feel for the first maple syrup of the season," says Bisson, serving a visitor a ladleful of maple reduction straight out of the vat. "We're the first ones to arrive at the market in March. When people see us, they smile. Maple syrup is gold to them. It is proof that we have survived another winter."

Dominique, France & René, St-Damase

Sirop d'érable
AMBRÉ
3 POUR 20.00
7.00 CH.

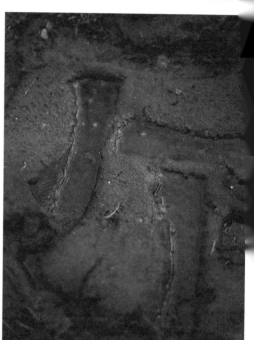

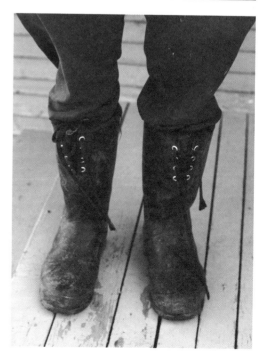

" *La tire*, we call it. Sticky, boiled-down maple taffy is poured over clean white snow. Twirl it around a popsicle stick and eat until it's all gone, except for the gummy amber threads tangled in your hair and your mitts."

Mousse à l'Érable

In Quebec, maple recipes are cherished heirlooms, handed down along with the silverware. Tante Aline shared this one from the Prud'homme family. A simple recipe calling for three ingredients, this mousse is like a cloud of maple taffy. But it is intensely sweet, so servings should be small. Shot glasses are just right.

(Serves 10)

1½ tsp powdered unflavoured gelatin (half an envelope)

1 cup (250 ml) maple syrup

¾ cup (180 ml) whipping cream

maple sugar and maple syrup, for garnish (optional)

In a small bowl, sprinkle gelatin evenly over 2 tbsp of water and stir until dissolved.

In a small saucepan, warm maple syrup. Slowly add gelatin, stirring to combine thoroughly. Refrigerate for 15 to 20 minutes, until cool but not chilled enough to set.

With a hand mixer, whip cream until stiff peaks form. Measure ¼ cup (50 ml) of whipped cream for garnish and set aside in refrigerator. Using a spatula, gently but thoroughly fold remaining whipped cream into cooled maple mixture.

Spoon into 2-oz (60 ml) shot glasses and refrigerate at least 90 minutes or until set. Top with a spoonful of whipped cream, a sprinkle of maple sugar and a drizzle of maple syrup and serve.

Maple Soy Duck Breast

Boneless duck breasts are easier to cook than whole duck. And with their meaty texture and deep flavour, they take well to this salty, sweet and peppery recipe. Duck breasts' thick layer of fat is rendered crispy and delicious when seared in a heavy pan over high heat, the sweet marinade caramelizing into a perfect crust.

Butcher Patrick Loyau likes the breasts, or *magrets*, of the Moulard duck best because they are larger and meatier than those of other ducks. At La Boucherie du Marché, he sells *magrets* that weigh 12 ounces (350 g) or more, enough for two people.

(*Serves 4*)

2 boneless duck breasts, skin on

2 tbsp coarsely ground black or green peppercorns

¼ cup (60 ml) soy sauce

½ cup (125 ml) maple syrup

2 tbsp finely grated fresh ginger

2 tsp vegetable oil

1/3 cup (80 ml) white wine

2 tbsp vinegar

Preheat oven to 325°F (160°C).

Using a sharp knife, score the skin side of the duck breasts in a cross-hatch pattern, cutting into the fat but being careful not to cut through to the meat. Season with pepper, rubbing into the meat on all sides.

In a shallow baking dish, combine soy sauce, maple syrup and grated ginger. Marinate duck breasts for at least 4 hours, or overnight. Remove duck breasts from marinade, reserving liquid. Drain and pat dry.

Heat oil in a heavy frying pan over high heat until oil is hot, but not smoking. Add duck breasts, skin side down, and lower heat to medium-high. Cook until the skin side is golden brown and crisp, about 8 to 10 minutes. Turn and sear the other side another 3 minutes. Remove duck breasts from the pan and transfer to oven for 10 minutes, covered loosely with foil.

Meanwhile, remove all but 2 tbsp of the fat from the frying pan. Over medium-high heat, add white wine and vinegar and deglaze the pan, bringing to a boil and scraping up the crispy bits until liquid is reduced by half. Add the reserved marinade and cook until slightly thickened, about 5 minutes. Slice each duck breast crosswise into ¼-inch-thick slices and pour the sauce over the meat. Serve on a platter atop gingered scallions or steamed bok choy drizzled with a little sesame oil.

Gingered Scallions

12 scallions, trimmed

2-inch (5 cm) piece fresh ginger, peeled

1 tbsp vegetable oil

Cut scallions in half lengthwise. Cut on the diagonal into slices about 3 inches (8 cm) long. Cut ginger into matchsticks.

Heat oil in a wok or frying pan until very hot but not smoking. Add scallions and ginger and fry over medium-high heat, without stirring, for 5 minutes or until onions are golden. Stir and continue cooking another 2 minutes or so.

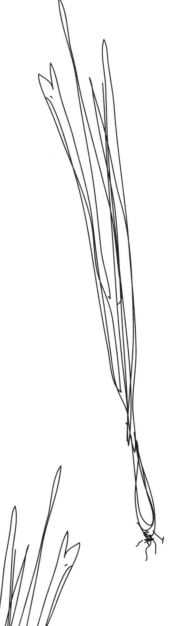

· THE FORAGER ·

François Lamontagne

François Lamontagne pushes back blackberry brambles and sloshes through a stream, soaking his pants to the knee. He's up a sandy riverbank and down a hillside, crunching through a carpet of dried leaves, pointing out trilliums and jack-in-the-pulpit, the early wildflowers of spring. He picks a mottled trout lily leaf and pops it into his mouth. Tastes like cantaloupe, he says. The bright-green shoots of wild day lilies are salad to him, too. Then Lamontagne stops, crouches and brushes away what looks like brown paper wrapping from a mound in the forest floor. There he finds what he came looking for: a clump of tight, green coils barely breaking through the damp ground. With a quick twist of the wrist he snaps a fiddlehead, brushes away its casing and drops it into his bucket.

Quebecers are crazy for *têtes de violons*, the spiral-shaped sprouts of the ostrich fern (*Matteuccia struthiopteris*), which grows wild across Quebec in forests and along riverbanks. There are hundreds of fern types, but only the ostrich fern's fiddleheads are edible. The picking season is short and intense, lasting only two or three weeks. Once the fern's large, exotic-looking leaves have formed, the plant is bitter and no longer edible.

Among the foragers who scour the forests in late April and early May, competition is fierce. Fiddleheads sell for $4 or $5 a pound, and a seasoned veteran like Lamontagne can pick $40 worth in an hour. When the fiddlehead season is over, he will be out for wild berries, cattails, wild ginger and mushrooms.

A forager's best sites are closely guarded secrets; some go so far as to blindfold hired pickers en route to the site. Lamontagne knows these woods near L'Épiphanie well. As a boy he and his cousin hunted partridge, rabbit and woodcock here. In a whole morning of searching and scraping, though, we have filled less than half a bag. Just the other day, Lamontagne picked 50 pounds at another spot. But he won't take us there.

François St-Jacques-de-Montcalm

Raw food ?
Not these

- - -

When buying fiddleheads, look for plump, bright-green, unblemished spirals that are tightly coiled. Wash them well under cold running water to clean them and remove their papery skins. If not using immediately, wrap them in a damp dishcloth and keep refrigerated, but not for more than a few days.

Fiddleheads absolutely must be cooked. They are indigestible and bitter, even toxic, when eaten raw. Boil or steam them for at least 8 minutes. Plunge in cold water to stop further cooking. Then eat them with a little salt and melted butter, or add them to omelettes or salads. They are also nice tossed with grated fresh ginger and soy sauce or served with hollandaise sauce alongside poached salmon.

Fiddleheads with Lemon Dressing

Fiddleheads are the true harbingers of spring in Quebec. Purists eat them boiled or steamed, just like that, but I like to jazz them up with a squirt of lemon and a little chili heat.

(Serves 4)

1 lb (500 g) fiddleheads, rinsed and trimmed

juice and finely grated zest of 1 lemon

¼ tsp dried red chili pepper

1 shallot, finely chopped

3 tbsp sunflower oil

salt

Steam fiddleheads for 8 to 10 minutes, then plunge into a bowl full of cold water to prevent further cooking. Drain and pat dry with a clean kitchen towel. In a medium bowl, whisk together remaining ingredients. Add fiddleheads and toss to coat. Serve warm or at room temperature.

· THE FISH FINDER ·

Christian Servant

Christian Servant can be elusive. One minute, he is there behind the counter at his fish store in Jean Talon Market, weighing whelks; the next minute he is outside, boiling crab.

Or he might be on his way back to the Gaspé. There, Servant is easy to pin down. Knock on the back door of his white clapboard house in Ste-Anne-des-Monts and there he is – in stocking feet at the dining room table, his laptop open, cellphone pressed to his ear, eyes on the St. Lawrence River shimmering endlessly before him as the sun burns through the fog. With the crab season over, he is on the lookout for turbot. Even from a distance, he can recognize José Servant's boat and know he will have whelks. If he spots Jean-Guy Vallée zigzagging outside his window, he calls him that evening to order scallops. Servant grew up on Gaspé's rugged north coast, and these fishermen are childhood friends.

Servant puts 75,000 kilometres a year on his Ford pickup truck transporting fish and seafood to Quebec City and Montreal. But first he finds it, and buys it. "You have to be there to get the best quality," Servant explains, racing down Highway 132 to the dock at Mont-Louis, his dog sprawled on the seat behind him. He has just had a call: a boat is coming in with 6,000 pounds of the turbot he wanted. His mission is to get there before the other buyers, to claim the freshest fish, not what has been at the bottom of the boat's hold for a day or two. Within 24 hours, the turbot he buys right there on the quay will be stacked in his counter at Les Délices de la mer. It will have been cleaned, filleted, packaged and shipped, along with salmon pies, marinated fish and coquilles St. Jacques that his mother and aunt prepare in their kitchen next door.

Servant says his customers ask a lot of questions about the fish they buy. "They want to know where the fish is from, how it lived, how it was fished," he says later in the evening, sipping wine as he flips lightly breaded turbot and ocean perch at the kitchen stove, the sun setting over the water in ribbons of pink, gold and coral. "That, I can tell them."

Christian, Mont-Louis, Saujerie

"Out of nowhere comes a brief, briny whiff of the sea. Am I dreaming? I follow a trail of drip marks down the hall. The rolling cart stops at the fishmonger's. The season's first crab has arrived."

La tourelle, Gaspésie

Eating crab...
Gaspé-style

The minute the ice melts in spring, the crabbing boats head out along the Gaspé Peninsula's north shore, lowering their colourful mesh and wire cages into the icy water at the mouth of the St. Lawrence River. The opening of *crabe des neiges* season in late March or early April is cause for celebration. These snow crabs with long, thin legs are the first catch of spring, along with shrimp from Matane.

Snow crab is most often sold already cooked, in sections consisting of four legs and a claw (that's where all the meat is) still in the bright-orange shell. Gaspesians prefer their crab *au naturel*. Not in crab cakes or bisques, not with cocktail sauce or a side dish of rice. Nothing, they insist, should get in the way of the soft, flaky texture of the meat and its sweet, briny taste. The sole exception is a regional specialty called *la délicieuse* – a triple-decker sandwich of crabmeat, sliced hard-boiled egg, mayonnaise, tomato and bacon.

Eating crab Gaspé-style is messy but fun. Tuck an apron or dishcloth at your neck and cover the table with newspaper. Get out a pile of napkins. Steam the crab briefly to reheat, or serve it cold. Pull the legs and claw off the cluster. Bend them at the joints and pull the sections apart, then pick out the tender filaments of meat with your fingers. Use scissors to cut through the shell if you need to. Dip the meat in plain melted butter, or add a squirt of lemon juice. Mayonnaise is also delicious. When you are done, wipe the sticky bits of crabmeat from your face.

Shrimp and Fennel Bisque

This velvety bisque plays the licorice notes of fennel and Pernod liqueur with the sweetness of shrimp. The recipe calls for cooked Matane shrimp, but any variety will do. If shrimp are raw, simply increase the cooking time by a few minutes.

(Serves 4)

2 tbsp butter

2 tbsp olive oil

1 large fennel bulb, thinly sliced (green fronds reserved for garnish)

2 leeks, white parts only, chopped

1 small onion, chopped

1/3 cup (80 ml) Pernod

4 cups (1 l) vegetable broth

1 large potato, peeled and cubed

1 lb (500 g) cooked, peeled Matane shrimp

white pepper

Heat olive oil and butter in a large saucepan. Add fennel, leeks and onion and cook over medium heat until soft but not coloured, about 5 minutes. Add Pernod, increase heat and cook briefly until liquid is reduced by half. Add vegetable broth and potato; simmer, covered, for 20 minutes or until potato is tender. Add shrimp and simmer 5 more minutes.

Cool slightly. Remove 8 shrimp from the pot and reserve for garnish.

In a blender, in small batches, purée the bisque until smooth and creamy. Taste and add salt, if necessary, and white pepper. Serve warm, garnished with reserved shrimp and chopped fennel fronds.

Shrimp from Quebec's shores

- - -

Nordic shrimp are the sweet, small, shockingly pink shrimp that we see in fish counters all year round. Best known as Matane shrimp, they have been cooked, peeled and frozen. Starting in mid-March, you can find the first of the Quebec catch at the market. These ones are still in their shells – heads, tails and all – and have not been frozen. They are a sign of the season.

Either way, Matane shrimp are usually cooked right on the boat or at the dock in Sept-Îles, on Quebec's Lower North Shore; or in Matane, on the northern coast of the Gaspé Peninsula. Wild and local, they are a great sustainable alternative to farmed shrimp imported from Thailand or China.

· THE ECOLOGIST ·

Mylène Dupont

When Mylène Dupont first turned up at the market, a young woman growing food organically, the old-timers looked at her scant bushels of zucchini with incomprehension. Little did they know how tough and determined she is.

Farming on six hectares of land in St-Eustache on loan from her parents, Dupont is a new breed of farmer. Certified organic, she doesn't use pesticides, fungicides or chemical fertilizers on the 60 different vegetables, fruits and flowers she grows, relying instead on crop rotation, chicken manure and ladybugs to do the work of enriching the soil and controlling harmful insects. No herbicides means hundreds of hours of back-breaking hoeing and weeding by hand. No pesticides means she must be hypervigilant for the first signs of insect infestations. Otherwise she risks losing an entire crop of leeks to voracious leek moth larvae, or a season's worth of red peppers to the devious little European corn borers who drill microscopic holes under the peppers' caps and feed, undetected, inside the fruit. It takes a detective's eye to see the minuscule piles of dust-like shavings they leave on the surface. For two summers straight when the rain never stopped, Dupont's yellow and striped zebra tomatoes were a writeoff, the fruit covered in unsightly black spots – blight fungus. She could have sprayed copper, but she wouldn't. Even though it is approved for use on organic produce, Dupont worries about the long-term effects of heavy-metal accumulation in the soil.

All wiry muscle, Dupont moves between rows of Lebanese cucumbers, wielding her hoe quickly and deftly to loosen the soil and uproot weeds. She pivots and twists, constantly changing position to prevent back injury. She makes sure to stretch, morning and night, and when all else fails she heads to the chiropractor. By midsummer, Dupont's tanned arms are muscled and taut and she feels strong and invincible, ready to balance 25-kilogram crates of melons against the belt buckle on her low-slung jeans.

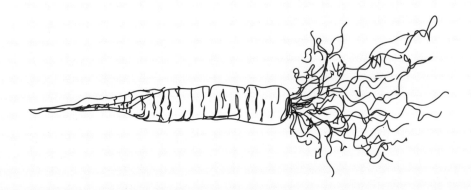

Mylène
Les Jardins
Mil'herbes

Spring Salad

The first hints of green out in the fields are baby lettuces and cool-weather arugula, pea shoots and watercress. They thrive in cool spring temperatures, bolting to seed when it gets too hot. Edible flowers like pansies, peppery nasturtiums and pink chive blossoms, too, make a spring appearance at the market, thanks to a head start in the greenhouse.

(Serves 4)
4 cups (1 l) mixed baby greens, washed and dried
½ cup (125 ml) thinly sliced radishes and/or baby white turnips
1 cup (250 ml) edible flowers
fleur de sel and freshly ground pepper

For vinaigrette:
¼ cup garlic scape pesto (see recipe)
2 tbsp white wine vinegar

In a large salad bowl, gently mix baby greens and sliced radishes. In a small bowl, make a vinaigrette by combining garlic scape pesto and vinegar. Add vinaigrette to salad and toss just to coat. Scatter with edible flowers and season with salt and pepper.

Garlic Scape Pesto

The stems of hardneck garlic are a treasure to cooks. Their corkscrew loops and subtle garlic flavour are fleeting springtime pleasures. Garlic growers snip them off to redirect the plant's energy to the bulb. The scapes, *fleurs d'ail*, are delicious chopped into omelettes or in a pesto brightened with lime juice – organic farmer Mylène Dupont's recipe for holding on to spring.

(Makes about 2 cups (500 ml))
2 cups (500 ml) chopped garlic scapes
½ tsp salt
juice of 1 large lime (about 3 tbsp)
1 cup (250 ml) sunflower oil

Purée garlic scapes, salt and lime juice. Add oil and mix. Transfer mixture to jars, leaving a space at the top. Add extra oil to completely cover the pesto. Tighten jars and refrigerate.

Asparagus and Goat Cheese Tart

Fresh, local asparagus makes its appearance in spring. The stalks are tender and the spears tightly closed. This golden puff pastry tart is nice hot or at room temperature.

(Serves 6 as an appetizer, 4 as a main course)

1 lb (500 g) asparagus, washed and trimmed

1 sheet prepared puff pastry, chilled (if frozen, make sure to thaw completely)

2 tsp olive oil

2 leeks, white parts only, thinly sliced

4 oz (115 g) soft unripened goat cheese

3 tbsp finely grated Parmesan cheese

1 egg, lightly beaten

¼ cup (60 ml) crème fraîche or sour cream

juice and finely grated zest of half a lemon

2 tsp fresh thyme leaves

sea salt and freshly ground pepper

Preheat oven to 425°F (220°C).

Fill a frying pan half full with water and bring to a boil. Add asparagus spears in a single layer and blanch for 2 minutes, until just tender. Drain immediately and rinse under cold water to prevent further cooking.

Line a baking sheet with parchment paper. On a lightly floured work surface, gently roll puff pastry sheet into a rectangle about 8 by 12 inches (20 by 30 cm). Slide dough onto the paper-lined baking sheet and fold each of the 4 edges to form a half-inch hem. Poke the middle of the pastry with a fork to prevent it from puffing up. Bake for 5 minutes, remove from oven and let cool.

Sauté leeks in 1 tsp of the olive oil until tender and translucent but not browned, about 5 minutes.

In a bowl, combine goat cheese, Parmesan cheese, beaten egg, crème fraîche, lemon juice, lemon zest and thyme. Spread pastry evenly with cheese mixture, then scatter with leeks. Top with asparagus spears. Brush everything with remaining 1 tsp of olive oil. Season with sea salt and pepper. Return to oven and bake for another 5 to 8 minutes, or until pastry is golden and crisp. Cut into squares and serve hot or at room temperature.

· THE EXPERIMENTALIST ·

Jacques Rémillard

Outside, it's 15 degrees Celsius — balmy for the middle of March in St-Michel-de-Napierville. In the greenhouse where Jacques Rémillard is in high gear planting herb cuttings, it is positively hot and steamy and his cheeks are flushed. Enveloped in a sea of spring green, he waters and tends his 50,000 snippings of rosemary, lavender or verbena until they take root. Soon, Rémillard, his wife Diane and son Patrick will have filled all nine of the greenhouses with potted herbs and vegetables for transplanting in backyard gardens and balcony pots across the city, as well as in his own fields when the danger of frost has passed. They are Rémillard's passion, these delicate seedlings. He pinches and rubs their leaves as he passes among them, raising his fingers to his nose to inhale their scent. Their names slip from his lips like lines in a love letter: melon sage, brandywine, black Russian, sanguine sorrel.

Rémillard is Jean Talon Market's resident experimentalist. He is a farmer with a flair for the exotic who has made a name for himself among gardeners and chefs for his novel and exciting produce. Sometimes, the new offerings are so unusual that no one recognizes them. So Rémillard gives them away — and bunch by bunch, basket by basket, he builds a following, as he did with his torpedo-shaped shallots or those now-ubiquitous tricoloured carrots he introduced more than a decade ago.

Rémillard spends his winters scouring online seed sites and poring over catalogues. He recruits travellers to far-off destinations to sneak a pack or two of the local seeds into their luggage. An Italian customer brought him a handful of seeds for friariello peppers from Naples, delicious for frying. Cuisses de poulet (chicken thigh) shallots arrived in a suitcase from Nice.

When a Ukrainian customer turns up looking for a rare heirloom parsnip, Rémillard's challenge is to find it and grow it. "It's awesome when they come back the next summer and I have it for them," he says, his handsome face breaking into a grin.

Jacques
au marché

Quick-Pickled Radishes

Sliced into translucent red-ringed circles, radishes are modern art. Their peppery kick pairs nicely with a sweet Asian vinaigrette. Don't toss them with the dressing, though, until right before serving or they go limp and soggy.

(Serves 2)

1 bunch radishes, washed and trimmed

2 tbsp sesame oil

1 tbsp rice vinegar

1 tsp sugar

1 tbsp freshly squeezed lime juice

1 tbsp finely grated fresh ginger

1 clove garlic, minced

salt and freshly ground pepper

2 tbsp toasted sesame seeds

¼ cup (60 ml) chopped chives

Using a mandoline or a sharp knife, slice radishes into very thin coins. Immerse in a bowl of cold water to keep them crisp.

In a medium bowl, combine sesame oil, rice vinegar, sugar, lime juice, ginger, garlic, salt and pepper. Drain radishes, pat dry and add to dressing. Sprinkle with sesame seeds and chives. Serve immediately.

Radish love

- - -

A bag of radishes has no romance. But a bunch of them – red, with long, scalloped leaves and trailing roots – is as pretty as a wedding bouquet. The French will set out a plate of red, pink or white-tipped radishes, an inch of green stem still attached, alongside a ramekin of cultured butter and a little bowl of fleur de sel. The cool, piquant bite of radish makes way for the creamy, sweet velvet of unsalted butter and the gentle crunch of sea salt. A radish haiku.

Rhubarb is so old-fashioned. There was a time when every garden had a patch. It's a perennial plant that grows just about anywhere. Market grower Michel Palardy is proudest of the Macdonald variety of rhubarb, developed in Montreal in the 1940s. It has fine-grained stalks, splendid flavour and intense red colour. Unlike other rhubarbs, it doesn't lose its ruby hue when cooked.

Rhubarb Fool

Sweetened cream and yogurt laced with tangy red rhubarb compote is heavenly. The compote is nice on its own, too, on toast for breakfast.

(Serves 4)

1 cup (250 ml) sugar

2 green cardamom pods, broken open

zest and juice of 1 large orange

4 cups (1 l) rhubarb, trimmed and cut into 1-inch (2.5 cm) pieces

½ cup (125 ml) whipping cream

½ cup (125 ml) plain yogurt

In a saucepan, combine sugar, cardamom, orange zest and juice with rhubarb; stir over medium heat until sugar is dissolved. Reduce heat to medium-low and simmer for 15 to 20 minutes or until rhubarb is soft and syrup is slightly thickened. Remove cardamom and allow to cool.

In a separate bowl, whip cream until stiff peaks form. Add yogurt and stir gently to combine. Fold in cooled rhubarb.

tournez à gauche sur cuillère.

Rue Paule aux Dessert et Gourmandise…

· THE NON-CONFORMIST ·

Anne Le

At first, there was tension behind the counter. A spring roll, Maman argued, should be made with nothing but rice noodles, shrimp or pork, lettuce and cucumber. Don't mess with Vietnamese tradition, she warned. But Anne Le couldn't help but experiment. She tried prosciutto from the charcuterie down the aisle, then spicy tuna. She introduced fresh mango and avocado, even marinated eggplant and arugula. Before long her summer kiosk at the market boasted 20 kinds of spring rolls. The international ingredients outraged Maman but dazzled the customers. At the end of each day, all 100 or 200 rolls they made would be sold. Maman had to relent.

Le's Vietnamese rolls are famous at the market for their translucent rice-paper wrappings and tantalizing fillings, each bite exploding with unexpected tastes and textures. They are, she says, a token of thanks to the city that saved her and a tribute to the woman who taught her to cook. Le was a scrawny 17-year-old from Hanoi living in a refugee camp in Singapore, her family wrenched apart by the Vietnam War. In 1978, her father made it to Montreal, one of a wave of Vietnamese "boat people" seeking asylum in Canada and the United States. A year later he sent for his youngest daughter and Le came to live in a crowded flat on St-Hubert St. with her father and two other Vietnamese refugees. She took French classes and looked for work, returning late in the afternoon to cook for the household. But what to make? Back home in Hanoi, her mother made an impressive repertoire of soups and rolls. But Le's mother had remained in Hanoi, along with her recipes. Here in Montreal, the women at the Buddhist temple guarded theirs jealously.

Except for Mui Thin, a Vietnamese woman of Chinese descent with no family of her own. She took young Le under her wing, fed her homemade rice cakes, and taught her the delicate art of assembling spring rolls. "Maman," Le came to call her mentor. In exchange, Le would accompany her to doctor's appointments and translate official documents.

When Le opened Les Délices d'Asie, her food stall at Jean Talon Market, Maman was there, too. And she still is. On their busiest days they sell hundreds of spring rolls and crispy fried imperial rolls.

Anne, Délices d'Asie

Vietnamese Spring Rolls

Moist and delicate, spring rolls are best eaten immediately, with the sweet and spicy dipping sauce *nuoc cham*. But they can also be wrapped individually in plastic and refrigerated for several hours.

(Makes 8 rolls)
4 oz (115 g) rice vermicelli
8 round rice-paper wrappers, 6- or 8½-inch diameter (15 or 20 cm)
12 large cooked shrimp, peeled, deveined and cut in half lengthwise
8 leaves Boston lettuce, washed and dried
handful of fresh mint leaves
handful of fresh coriander
handful of fresh Thai basil
½ cucumber, peeled and cut into slivers
hoisin peanut sauce (see recipe)

Bring a medium-size pot of water to a boil, then remove from heat and add rice noodles. Leave them to soak 2 or 3 minutes to soften slightly. Drain immediately and set aside.

Fill a large, shallow bowl with lukewarm water. One at a time, immerse the rice paper wrappers in the water for a few seconds, just until softened. Wet them completely, but do not let the wrappers soak too long or they will begin to disintegrate.

Work one spring roll at a time. Lay the moistened wrapper on a clean work surface and leave for a minute to soften a little more, until easy to work with. On the bottom third of each wrapper, lay 3 shrimp halves. Top with a lettuce leaf, noodles, fresh herbs and cucumber. Drizzle with a spoonful of hoisin-peanut sauce.

Begin rolling up the roll, then fold the sides in and continue rolling. Transfer to a serving platter, shrimp side up. Cover loosely with a clean, damp dishtowel to prevent drying. Continue until all wrappers have been filled. Serve immediately, accompanied by small bowls of *nuoc cham*.

Hoisin Peanut Sauce

½ cup (125 ml) smooth peanut butter
½ cup (125 ml) hoisin sauce
4 tbsp warm water

Blend the peanut butter, hoisin sauce and water, stirring well to combine. If too thick, add more water.

Nuoc Cham

1/3 cup (80 ml) sugar
3 tbsp rice vinegar
3 tbsp freshly squeezed lime juice
3 tbsp water
1/3 cup (80 ml) Asian fish sauce
1 Thai chili pepper, very finely chopped

In a small bowl, combine all ingredients and stir until sugar is dissolved.

- Feel free to play -

Light Vietnamese rolls (see recipe, facing page) are called *goi cuon*, which means
mixed salad roll. Translucent rice-paper wrappers are filled with shrimp or pork
(or both), plus rice vermicelli, raw vegetables and fresh herbs. Never fried, they
are served at room temperature with a dipping sauce.

Anne Le's spring rolls at Jean Talon Market are bursting with exuberant flavour.
She is not afraid to experiment with fillings like prosciutto, avocado, grilled
eggplant and smoked salmon.

· THE HEIR ·

Steven Finkelstein

For four decades, Jeno Finkelstein ruled the roost. At 5:30 every morning, he took up his position at his stall, selling chickens, live and squawking, from the family farm in St-Zotique. Later, when the market disallowed the sale of live animals, he sold just the eggs the hens laid. His market day began hours before the first customer arrived. There were eggs to sort and repack. And competitors to keep an eye on. Le Capitaine, they called him, a nod to the ship captain's hat that was Finkelstein's trademark and to his status as the market's longest-serving vendor. Some thought him rough and prickly, but at Le Capitaine's funeral, the chapel was packed to overflowing with customers and competitors.

Steven was just a kid when he started pitching in at the market, after school and all day Saturday. Nobody forced him to come. But he had listened to his parents' tales of dangerous escape from Hungary after the revolution. He felt duty-bound to help. As a grown man with a teaching job of his own, Steven kept coming to the market, doing double duty after work and on weekends. When his father turned 75 and began to flag, Steven took over the weekend shifts altogether.

"He worked hard and he expected us to, too. He made sure everyone knew exactly who was boss," says Steven, quiet-spoken, with a gentle porcelain face. He is perched behind the wooden counter, wrapping a customer's cartons of eggs in yesterday's newspaper.

"Really, it was my father's whole life," says Finkelstein as he looks over the day's supply of organic, free-range chicken eggs, plus big turkey and duck eggs, and quail eggs no bigger than a thimble. "He loved everything about this market, the constant flow of customers, the rumble of trucks, even the haggling with people who offered $4.50 for a $5 carton of eggs."

In the end, Finkelstein Sr. found a fitting way to reward his dutiful son. He willed the business, Le Capitaine, to Steven. And now those neatly stacked trays of eggs in all sizes, the outdoor kiosk that moves indoors for winter, and the faithful customers who return every week for their cartons of eggs are Steven's life. "I love it here. I always have," he says.

Steven, Le Capitaine

Baked Moroccan Omelette

A spongy, family-size omelette like this one has more in common with a *tortilla española* or an Italian frittata than a delicate French omelette. It is perfect for brunch, lunch or a light supper, eaten warm or at room temperature. Tuck the leftovers into a crusty roll for a delicious sandwich the next day.

To go with it, make a simple salad of grated carrots dressed with lemon juice, olive oil, chopped parsley and pinches of cumin and sweet paprika. Or cucumber, red onion and diced tomato with lemon juice and fresh mint. Chopped pitted dates and cut-up orange is another option. Or all of the above – they are classic Moroccan side dishes.

(Serves 6 to 8)

2 cups (500 ml) peeled, cubed potatoes (about 2 large potatoes)
1 cup (250 ml) chopped carrots (about 2 carrots)
3 tbsp extra-virgin olive oil
¼ cup (60 ml) chopped coriander leaves
¼ cup (60 ml) chopped parsley leaves
½ tsp ground turmeric
salt and freshly ground pepper
12 eggs

Preheat oven to 350°F (180°C).
Place potatoes and carrots in a medium saucepan filled with cold water. Bring to a boil, reduce heat and simmer 15 to 20 minutes, until vegetables are tender. Drain, then mash until smooth and lump-free. Oil a 9-by-13-inch (3.5 l) baking dish or 9-inch round (1.5 l) casserole and place in the preheated oven for several minutes.

Add olive oil, coriander, parsley and turmeric to potato-carrot mixture and mix well. Season to taste with salt and pepper. Add eggs, 2 at a time, mixing well with a wooden spoon after each addition. Remove baking dish from oven and transfer omelette mixture into it. Bake for 30 to 40 minutes until centre of omelette is set and top is golden brown. Cut into squares or wedges and serve warm or at room temperature.

Egg esoterica

– – –

Steven Finkelstein sells all sizes of chicken egg at the market. But there is more. Turkey eggs, looking like they were layed by pterodactyls, weigh up to four ounces each. It takes a mallet to crack open their thick, brown-speckled shells.

Duck eggs are pale blue-green, with oversized orange yolks and viscous whites. Bakers love them for the silky texture they lend custards and the deep colour they add to cakes. (Use one duck egg for every two chicken eggs.)

Teeny quail eggs, the size of foil-wrapped chocolate Easter eggs, have exquisite brown, black and grey mottling. They have a lighter, sweeter taste than chicken eggs. Quail eggs are a delicacy in places like Japan, where they are used raw in sushi, and Scandinavia, where they are hard-boiled and sliced over smoked fish.

Œufs de dinde, de cane, de poule et de caille

"How to shop at the market: Come with an appetite but leave the grocery list at home. Get lost. Ask questions. What does that taste like? How do you cook this? Where does it grow? Let the season set the menu."

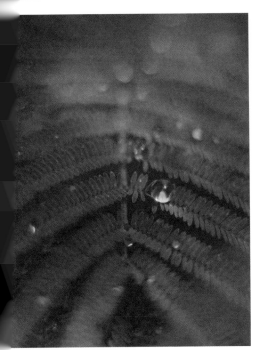

· Le Chocolatier ·

Ludovic Fresse

If he had a spare moment, Ludovic Fresse might pause to give thanks to the pagan goddess of spring, Eostre. The early Christians named Easter after her, adopting her fondness for baby animals and eggs. Now it isn't Easter without chocolate bunnies and candy-filled eggs.

But the *chocolatier* is too busy for that. In his atelier with its vats of melting cocoa and cream, Fresse and a crew of 12 will have fashioned more than 16,000 Easter animals by the time Sunday rolls around. They go home at night, their aprons smeared with chocolate, and dream about rabbits, ducks and chicks. This is the busiest week of the year at Chocolats Privilège, and the sweet smell of Belgian, Tanzanian and Madagascar chocolate fills the air.

"Easter used to be rooted in religion," says Fresse, who worked as a pastry chef in his native France, then in Luxembourg and the United States, before training in Montreal as a *chocolatier*. "But now it's all about chocolate." Some years on Good Friday, they have had to work right through the night to refill the shelves in Fresse's market shop with chocolate animals in 300 different shapes and sizes.

Fresse's creations are elaborate, each one moulded by hand and individually painted with layers and layers of white and dark chocolate detailing. They are then filled with melted milk chocolate and left to drip on racks before being chilled and unmoulded. The mode in Paris these days is for sleek, high-design confections. But at Fresse's Montreal workshop, Easter is for children. The squirrels he creates feature fuzzy white chocolate "fur" applied with an airbrush; the bunnies have life-like eyes; the glossy milk-chocolate hens with etched feathers sit in packages padded with grass nests. "To me, they aren't Easter chocolates unless they look at you and call 'Eat me, eat me,'" Fresse says.

Ludovic, à la chocolaterie

Sorbets
citron • framboise • lulo
mangue • pamplemousse
cassis • poire et cidre
bissap • melon • masala chai
mango malai • fraises de l'île

Glaces
vanille • choco 72% • chocolait
noisette • pistache • coco
expresso • dulce de leche
caramel brûlé à l'érable
marron • matcha

– SUMMER –

(Grow)

....

Out in the street, the July sun beats down mercilessly. Montreal is sweltering in a five-alarm heat wave. But here in the shade of the market's old cement canopy, it feels almost cool. A toddler, face smeared with chocolate ice cream, perches on his father's shoulders. A tattooed teenager drags over a hose and douses herself, then the wilting tomato plants at her family's stall. Oxygenated by all the greenery, the air seems fresher. Amid the pots of herbs and flowers and bushels of leafy greens, it is almost possible to forget the sticky asphalt and the steamy bus ride along Jean Talon St.

Bees and wasps and picky old ladies buzz about in search of the choicest plums and squash blossoms. There is nothing the rich, black fields that ring the city won't hand over. The tomatoes are off the vine, sweet corn comes in by the truckload every day. Even before the watermelons are done, the first apples have made their debut.

At the Birri Brothers stall, the peppers are not just red and green, but purple, orange, black, chartreuse. There are prickly little cukes for pickling and long-stemmed, feathery bouquets of camomile and dill flower, garlands of red-hot chilis hung to dry.

The pageant opens with the first strawberries of mid-June, followed by raspberries, blackberries and ground cherries. One week the sour cherries suddenly appear – and disappear – and then it is time for lobster from les Îles-de-la-Madeleine. Blueberries give way to dusty purple plums, and so the summer unfolds.

Quebec's pride in this embarrassment of riches is on display across the market. *"Frais du Québec"* proclaim the handwritten signs at every stall. *"De chez nous."* *"100% Québec."* By August, the market is at full throttle. Farmers work 16-hour days, getting their harvest in, dodging rush-hour traffic to deliver it. Nathalie Trottier has hardly seen her husband in weeks. She's here at their market stall. He's back home on the berry farm working the fields. There's time for a quick peck on the cheek at 5 a.m., as he stumbles into bed after an overnight delivery – just as she gets up to go.

On a sweaty Saturday afternoon, it seems that all of Montreal is here at the market, with dogs, babies and grandparents in tow. It takes sharp elbows and a purposeful stride to cut through the crowds until a flash thunderstorm rolls across the sky, sending down a torrent of hail and rain, dispersing the shoppers. And then it is cool and quiet for a while.

Hot, hot, hot. Summertime and the living is easy.

077

· THE STRAWBERRY SAVANT ·

Daniel Racine

A strawberry is not just a strawberry. Not if you are Daniel Racine, who plants a dozen different varieties in the fields behind his bungalow. "At the grocery store, they just call them strawberries. They don't know what variety they are, whether they are good for jam or better for freezing," says Racine with disdain as he bends along a straw-lined path to pick enormous, juicy Cabots, the perfect strawberries for shortcake. "They don't even care."

His parents were vegetable farmers who sent him to private school hoping he would find a job that paid better, with shorter hours. But he didn't. Instead, he took over the 16-acre family farm in Ste-Anne-des-Plaines, northwest of Montreal, and turned it into a farm specializing in strawberries and raspberries — one of only a handful left in this town once billed as the strawberry capital of Quebec. He hopes his four children will take the reins one day, even if it means staying up nights in May and early June, in case the sprinklers need to be turned on to protect tender white blossoms from frost. Even if it means seven days a week of back-breaking work the rest of the summer, hand-weeding and fertilizing the fields, harvesting berries and getting them to market the same day.

At Racine's stall, Quebec strawberries are jewels, each with its own pedigree and purpose. Unlike their imported cousins, his berries aren't shipped thousands of kilometres. They aren't bred and selected for travel-hardiness, but rather for flavour, colour, juiciness and yield. And they are picked only when ripe, which makes them so intoxicatingly fragrant and sweet. The long-awaited local strawberry season opens with the Veestar, a tiny, dark-fleshed, sublimely delicious but extremely delicate berry, best eaten right away. Next comes Wendy, big and buxom but not as sweet. Then the jumbo Cabot, and Jewel, Quebec's most widely cultivated strawberry, firm and bright red, the quintessential jam-making berry. Later come Mesabi, the vanilla-scented, rose-coloured Harmony, and finally Saint-Laurent d'Orléans, the last hurrah.

Daniel, Ste-Anne-des-Plaines

Ferme Racine, Ste-Anne-des-Plaines

Rhu-berry Jam

This is an easy, small-batch recipe for strawberry rhubarb jam. Because the filled jars are not heat-processed, they must be refrigerated. Be sure to wash and sterilize the jars, lids and utensils in boiling water for 15 minutes before using.

4 cups (1 l) hulled, sliced strawberries

4 cups (1 l) coarsely chopped rhubarb

3 cups (750 ml) sugar

2 tbsp vinegar or fresh lemon juice

1 tbsp butter

Combine strawberries, rhubarb, sugar and vinegar or lemon juice in a large, heavy saucepan over medium-high heat. Bring to a full, rolling boil, then reduce heat to medium-low. Add butter to prevent foaming. Cook, stirring regularly, until fruit is softened and jam thickens, about 30 to 40 minutes.

To test if jam has set, place a small spoonful on a chilled plate. If the jam holds when the plate is inverted, it is ready. If it is still runny, return to stovetop for another few minutes. With a clean spoon, transfer hot jam into still-hot sterilized jars, leaving a half-inch (1 cm) headspace. Wipe rims with a clean cloth. Screw on lids. Allow to cool to room temperature, then refrigerate.

Strawberry Nutella Pizza

All dressed, for dessert. The crust is no-fail cookie dough, topped with mascarpone cream and fresh strawberries, then drizzled with Nutella cream.

(Serves 8)

For cookie crust:

1 cup (250 ml) butter, softened

1 cup (250 ml) sugar

1 egg

1 tsp vanilla

2 tsp baking powder

2¾ cups (680 ml) flour

For mascarpone cream:

2 cups (500 ml) mascarpone cheese

1/3 cup (80 ml) icing sugar

1 tsp freshly squeezed lemon juice

1 tbsp Cointreau or other orange-flavoured liqueur

1 tsp vanilla

For strawberries:

2 cups (500 ml) hulled, thickly sliced strawberries

2 tbsp sugar

For Nutella cream:

¼ cup (60 ml) Nutella chocolate hazelnut spread

2 tbsp 35 per cent cream

Preheat oven to 400°F (200°C).

In a large bowl, cream butter and sugar until fluffy. Beat in egg and vanilla. Add baking powder and flour, 1 cup at a time, mixing after each addition. Gather the dough and divide it into 2 balls. Wrap one in plastic wrap and refrigerate or freeze for future use. On a floured surface, roll the other ball into a large disk and transfer to an ungreased 12-inch (30 cm) pizza pan, pressing the dough to the edges. Bake 15 minutes or until edges are lightly browned. Remove from oven and cool on rack. Do not remove crust from pizza pan.

Whisk together mascarpone, icing sugar, lemon juice, liqueur and vanilla. Refrigerate. In another bowl, combine strawberries and sugar and let stand 30 minutes. Meanwhile, heat Nutella and cream in the top of a double boiler until melted. Stir to combine and let cool slightly.

Spread mascarpone cream on cooled cookie crust. Pile on strawberries and drizzle with Nutella cream.

· THE PRODIGAL SON ·

Giancarlo Sacchetto

Where Giancarlo Sacchetto comes from, pasta isn't something mass-produced, bagged in cellophane and stocked at the supermarket next to the ready-made sauces. In Torino, in northern Italy, where his family lived when he was a boy, every neighbourhood had its own *pastificio* – a small, traditional pasta factory where pasta was made fresh daily, by hand. It was in such a *pastificio* that his father, Giuseppe Sacchetto, spent years learning the secrets of artisanal pasta. When he emigrated to Montreal with his family in the mid-1970s, he went into business for himself in the city's north end. As word spread about the Sacchettos' infinite variety of handmade pastas, their plump meat- and cheese-filled ravioli and authentic, yellow-toned tagliolini, the lineups outside their Casa dei Ravioli grew. Before long it was a temple within the Italian community.

The pasta-maker's son, Giancarlo, helped out as a teenager. But he loved airplanes, and he craved a career of his own. For 15 years he worked as an aeronautical technologist. Pasta was what he ate, not what he did. But when Sacchetto Sr. became ill and had to step aside, his son felt a pull back into the family fold. He took over the business, learning from scratch his father's secrets. "I had my notebook to write it all down," Sacchetto recalled. "But my father had no measurements, it was all in his hands. 'Dad, Dad, what did you just put in there?' I would ask. 'It's up to you to watch more closely,' he would reply."

Day after day, Sacchetto continued his apprenticeship, his father standing over him, sprinkling more oregano on the meat when needed, pointing out the moment when the dough reached perfect elasticity. Then, just as his father had, Sacchetto opened his own *pastificio*, a busy shop in the market where customers who arrive first thing in the morning can watch him mixing the dough according to his father's recipes. On Sundays, the shop is filled with the aroma of simmering sauces and braising beef and veal, the ingredients for the following day's ravioli and tortellini stuffing. On Tuesdays, paper-thin sheets of pasta are cut into long ribbons of fettuccine, spaghetti and tagliolini.

Sometimes Sacchetto steps out into the market aisle outside Pastificio Sacchetto, proudly proffering samples of pumpkin-filled ravioli or meat-filled mezzelune, just made. He has won awards for his pasta. He supplies some of the best restaurants in town. People tell him he makes the best ravioli they have ever eaten. It hasn't gone to his head, though. "Pasta is artisanal work. You are never quite finished learning."

Giancarlo, al Pastificio

Cherry Tomato & Mozzarella Pasta

This summer pasta with its barely cooked sauce is a favourite of pasta-maker Giancarlo Sacchetto. It takes no time at all, since the tomatoes don't need peeling or seeding and the fresh pasta cooks in a couple of minutes. Sacchetto's secret to silky sauce is fresh mozzarella cheese and a knob of butter tossed in just before serving.

(Serves 4)

4 tbsp extra-virgin olive oil

1 medium onion, finely chopped

2 large cloves garlic, crushed

2 lb (1 kg) cherry tomatoes, cut in half

salt and freshly ground pepper

1 cup (250 ml) fresh basil leaves, shredded

8 oz (225 g) fresh mozzarella cheese, drained and coarsely chopped

1 lb (500 g) fresh fettuccine or tagliatelle

1 tbsp butter

freshly grated Parmesan cheese

crushed red chili peppers (optional)

Bring a large pot of generously salted water to a boil.

Heat olive oil in a saucepan over medium heat. Add onion and cook, stirring occasionally, until translucent. Add garlic and continue cooking for another minute. Add cherry tomatoes, salt and pepper. Raise the heat to medium-high and cook, stirring occasionally, until the tomatoes break up and become saucy, about 10 to 15 minutes. Turn off heat. Add basil and mozzarella cheese and stir to combine.

Meanwhile, cook the pasta until it is al dente — tender but firm. (With fresh pasta, this will only take 2 or 3 minutes.) Drain immediately.

In a large serving bowl, toss together hot pasta and tomato sauce. Add butter and stir to combine. Serve with Parmesan cheese and crushed chili peppers, if desired.

· THE HEDONIST ·

Robert Lachapelle

On sultry summer evenings, when it is hotter in Montreal than in Cairo, the lineups snake out the door of Havre aux Glaces and around the corner. The rest of the market is dark and quiet, but Robert Lachapelle's devotees just keep coming. They can't help themselves. Each cool, creamy mouthful is a jolt of flavour, a hit of sublime pleasure.

Lachapelle's sorbets and ice creams are made from natural, seasonal ingredients plucked straight from nearby market stalls, then pulsed, spun and chilled right there in the shop. They have spawned a cult following.

Sensualists crave his dark-chocolate ice cream with *piment d'Espelette*, or dream about the ephemeral fruitiness of his pear and port creation. There are those who close their eyes and moan at the first sweet-tangy taste of his Tarocco blood orange sorbet. "Maybe it's the colours, or the feeling that ice cream evokes in people. Their muscles relax and their pupils dilate. Their faces lighten and they sigh," Lachapelle says. "But I get pleasure, too. From seducing people, surprising them."

It was his own seduction, on a beach in Belize, that brought him here to this shop in the market. For most of his career, Lachapelle was a corporate tax planner. Then he and his wife took a year's sabbatical to explore the Caribbean Sea with their two small boys. They bought a 37-foot yacht and sailed to the Bahamas, making their way to Cuba and El Salvador, Honduras and Guatemala, snorkelling and fishing, eating tropical fruit from outdoor markets. It was an ice cream vendor in Belize making mango sorbet – orange and fresh and exploding with flavour – who sparked the idea for Lachapelle's new life. Upon his return to Montreal he ditched his job, bought a sorbet machine, signed up for ice cream classes and pitched a business plan to the market. Now, with his brother Richard as a partner, he mans the deck at Havre aux Glaces, a long and narrow space reminiscent of a sailing vessel.

"This place is my ship and the market is my quay," he says, his hair tousled, legs in Capri pants dangling from a stool outside the shop as a languid Thursday afternoon rolls to an end.

Roberto
Havrelana Glaces

Negroni Glacé

The negroni is an iconic aperitif from Florence. As Orson Welles said, "The bitters are excellent for your liver, the gin is bad for you. They balance each other." For the bitters, use Campari or Aperol, or the non-alcoholic Stappjno.

(Serves 1)
1 scoop orange sorbet
½ oz (15 ml) gin
1 oz (30 ml) Italian bitters
freshly squeezed lemon juice
thin wedge of orange

Spoon sorbet into a small glass and add gin, bitters and a splash of lemon juice. Garnish with orange wedge. Stir and sip.

Frozen Strawberry Daiquiri

Here's an icy riff on an old Cuban classic.

(Serves 1)
1 scoop strawberry sorbet
1 oz (30 ml) dark rum
½ lime
1 strawberry slice

Place sorbet in a small glass and pour rum over it. Squeeze in lime juice. Garnish with strawberry slice. Stir and sip.

Sgroppino

They drink this frothy drink after dinner in Venice.

(Serves 2)
1 cup (250 ml) lemon sorbet
½ cup (125 ml) prosecco or other sparkling wine
1 oz (30 ml) vodka
2 thin half-slices of lemon

Working quickly with a whisk, whip together sorbet, prosecco and vodka in a bowl just until frothy. (Don't overmix or it will melt.) Pour into frosted champagne flutes or glasses. Garnish with lemon and serve immediately.

- Cocktails Glacés -

An icy cocktail is the most effective coolant on a sweltering summer evening. Robert Lachapelle, from Havre aux Glaces, chills out with sparkling prosecco splashed over sweet-tart lemon sorbet. Or maybe a scoop of espresso ice cream with Bailey's Irish Cream.

Serve cocktails glacés in glass verrines, shot glasses, champagne flutes or liqueur glasses. They can be blended beforehand like slushies or assembled right in the glass. Stir and sip, or eat with a little demitasse spoon.

· THE STOIC ·

Yvon Huard

It takes more than a bout of bad weather to make a Gaspesian fisherman complain. Yvon Huard's hands are raw and cracked, his rubber overalls crusted in mud. He has been fishing since he was 12 and by now he is impervious to rain, gnawing damp and other meteorological extremes.

He and his son Stéphane rose at 2 a.m., as they have nearly every day since the end of April, when the lobster season opened here in the Baie des Chaleurs, in the frigid, shallow waters off the Gaspé Peninsula's south coast. Normally, the lobstermen are out on the water long before sunrise and home again by mid-morning, having followed a trail of colourful buoys to their 235 lobster traps. But thick-knit fog kept them land-bound until noon. Then fierce winds rocked the boat so violently it was a battle just hoisting the traps in and out of the water.

So it is almost four in the afternoon by the time the Huards have transferred four large crates of lobster, more than 100 pounds, to the wholesaler's truck waiting on the dock in Newport, bound in a day or so for landlocked markets like Jean Talon. They are getting $4 a pound this season, and the catch is up. Just last year, the lingering recession in the United States sent prices plummeting to under $3 a pound, the lowest in 30 years.

Huard can still remember the panic that took along these winding shores in the early 1990s. That was when Atlantic groundfish stocks all but disappeared and the government closed the cod fishery, putting an end to the region's largest industry. It had been in place even before Jacques Cartier landed here in 1534. "But we adapted. We survived," he says in his slow, thick Baie des Chaleurs drawl. "It's what you do when you live from the sea."

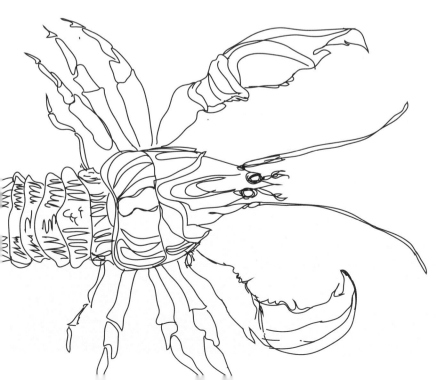

Yvon, Newport, Gaspésie

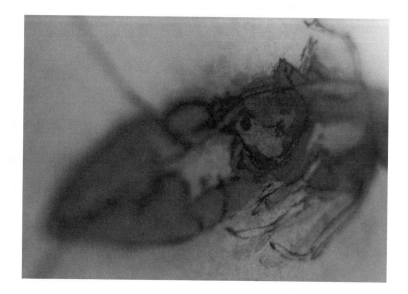

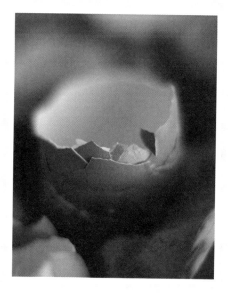

Lobster Roll - *Guédille*

The arrival of Quebec lobster, fished from the Baie des Chaleurs off Gaspé's southern coast and from les Îles-de-la-Madeleine, sparks a city-wide celebration with every second restaurant heralding its own *festival du homard*.

The Gaspé version of the classic New England lobster roll is called a *guédille*. It calls for a hot dog bun and cooked lobster meat (or shrimp) with jarred mayonnaise.

My adaptation of the *guédille* is served on sourdough baguette slathered with homemade aioli. The zesty mayonnaise features lemon and garlic – lobster's two favourite accompaniments.

(Serves 2 or 3)
1 sourdough baguette
¼ cup (60 ml) lemon garlic aioli (see recipe)
2-lb (1 kg) lobster, cooked and shelled
1 cup (250 ml) salad greens, washed and dried
½ cup (125 ml) sliced marinated hot peppers

Slice baguette open lengthwise. Slather bottom half with aioli. Cut cooked lobster pieces into thick slices and lay over the aioli. Top with salad greens and hot pepper slices. Cover with top half of baguette and slice into 2 or 3 servings.

Lemon Garlic Aioli

Making your own mayonnaise is easier than you think. The key is making sure the eggs are at room temperature and the oil is added slowly.

1 egg
1 egg yolk
1 cup (250 ml) sunflower oil
salt and freshly ground pepper
2 tbsp freshly squeezed lemon juice
2 cloves garlic, crushed
¼ cup (60 ml) finely chopped fresh chives

In a food processor, whir together the egg and egg yolk and 3 tbsp oil. With the food processor running, add remaining oil in a slow stream, only a spoonful at a time. The mixture will slowly thicken. Transfer to a bowl and add salt and pepper, lemon juice, garlic and chives, stirring to combine. If necessary, adjust seasonings. Use immediately or cover and store in the refrigerator. Aioli is at its best when eaten within a few hours.

"Even after all these years, I still get lost in the market's labyrinth. I never mind, though. Take a wrong turn and you end up behind a stall where the workers are rinsing dirt from bunches of coriander. The next thing you know, you're in search of avocado and a lime for guacamole."

Sour Cherry Cobbler

I have a soft spot for rustic cobblers, baked in cast iron pans, served warm with ice cream. Any fruit will do.

(Serves 8)
For fruit filling:
4 cups (1 l) sour cherries, washed and pitted
½ cup (125 ml) sugar
3 tbsp cornstarch

For batter:
1/3 cup (80 ml) butter, softened
½ cup (125 ml) sugar
1 egg
2/3 cup (160 ml) buttermilk
1½ cups (375 ml) flour
1½ tsp baking powder
pinch of salt

Preheat oven to 400°F (200°C).
Toss sour cherries with sugar and cornstarch and let stand for 10 minutes. Transfer to a greased 10-inch (25 cm) cast iron pan or 13-by-9-inch (3.5 l) baking dish.

In a large bowl, cream butter and sugar until fluffy. Beat in egg, then add buttermilk. Add flour, baking powder and salt and beat again, just until mixed.

Drop batter onto cherries in spoonfuls, not entirely covering the fruit. Bake 45 minutes, or until fruit is bubbly, topping is golden and a wooden skewer inserted into it comes out clean. Cool slightly and serve with ice cream.

Cherry amour

Old-fashioned sour cherries – with their tart flavour, Valentine's Day colour and almond bouquet – are the most ephemeral of early summer's treasures. Out of nowhere, a few baskets turn up amid the strawberries and redcurrants at Réal Alary's market stand, but only for a week or so at the end of June or in early July. Unlike those showy, deep-garnet Bing cherries we know so well, sour cherries aren't trucked in from Washington or British Columbia. There is a variety called Montmorency that is entirely local, hardy enough to grow in Quebec. Known as *griottes* in French, they are perfect for pies and other desserts, holding their shape better than sweet cherries. They freeze well, too.

Once upon a time, there was a sour cherry tree on every farm, its snow-white blossoms putting on a spectacular springtime show. But few farmers still keep Montmorency trees. The season is short-lived and the fruit is highly perishable. Alary himself has only four sour cherry trees left back on the farm in Ste-Anne-des-Plaines. Every year, it's a race to get out the ladders and pick the fruit before the blackbirds clear every last branch.

Griottes. Sucrées. Surettes. La joie !

salsa

Pico de Gallo

"The rooster's beak" is what this Mexican salsa is called in Spanish. Tomatoes, onion and coriander are chopped by hand, never puréed. It can go from mild to numbingly hot. This recipe is medium-hot. Adjust the amount of habanero pepper to your taste, leaving it out altogether for a perfectly mild salsa.

4 medium tomatoes, chopped
1 medium Spanish onion, chopped
½ bunch fresh coriander, finely chopped
juice of 2 limes
pinch of dried oregano
salt and freshly ground pepper
1 habanero pepper, very finely chopped

Combine all ingredients in a medium bowl. Let stand half an hour. This salsa is best eaten within an hour or two.

Tomatillo Salsa

Green tomatillos have a pleasant tang that gives this green salsa its citrus note. For best flavour, look for smaller ones. Soak them in cold water for a few minutes to help remove the sticky brown casings.

15 tomatillos, halved
2 small shallots, peeled
1 bunch coriander, washed and stems removed
2 small jalapeno peppers, seeded
4 cloves garlic
1 tsp dried oregano
salt and freshly ground pepper

Reserve several sprigs of coriander for garnish. In a blender or food processor, purée all the ingredients until smooth. Let stand at least half an hour to allow flavours to blend. Serve in a bowl garnished with coriander leaves.

Black Bean Salsa

Roasting corn in its husk adds a smoky, caramel-like dimension to this salsa. Even frozen kernels can be pan-fried until golden to coax out their personality.

2 cups (500 ml) roasted corn
½ cup (125 ml) finely chopped red onion
1 19-ounce (540 ml) can black beans, rinsed and drained
1 tsp ground cumin
1 large tomato, chopped
2 cloves garlic, crushed
3 tbsp chopped fresh coriander
1 tsp chipotle in adobo sauce, chopped
2 tbsp freshly squeezed lime juice

Combine all ingredients in a medium bowl. Let stand at least 30 minutes for flavours to blend.

El Rey del Taco

Javier Muñoz is king of the taco. At El Rey del Taco, you'll find him behind the grill, engulfed in the meaty aromas of pork, beef and chicken spiced with epazote, coriander and oregano

Outside on the patio in front of his restaurant at the market, salsa music pulses from the speakers. The cooks assemble *gorditas* – cornmeal tortillas stuffed with shredded pork, guacamole and smoked peppers pounded to a paste. The *churros*, pillows of fried dough sprinkled with sugar, are dangerously addictive.

And as promised, Muñoz's tacos are majestic, slathered in his famous salsas.

· THE ITALIANS ·

Lino & Bruno Birri

It's always a scene at the Birri Brothers stall. A woman in polka-dot stilettos and a six-inch skirt is buying peppers and Frank Baldassarre, his blond hair tied in a ponytail, gets up close to take her order. "Ciao sweetheart, how are you my love?" he asks, pouring on the charm. Baldassarre, the stall's longtime manager, swears he is this attentive with all the customers. And indeed, the next shopper, an old woman in orthopedic shoes, gets a big hug and his undivided attention as she picks eggplants for her parmigiana. Everybody who enters the Birri Brothers burgundy canopy is welcomed into the family.

Lino Birri, a reserved man with silver hair and endless patience, is here by 6 a.m., instructing the young workers. His brother Bruno is in the back, inspecting the day's deliveries. Lino and Bruno grew up on Drolet St. in Little Italy. The brothers weren't even 10 years old when they started working at the market. Their father had been badly injured in a work accident and the boys were called on to help their mother make ends meet.

Soon enough, Lino and Bruno had started their own business. They bought a parcel of land in Laval and built a couple of greenhouses, where they would grow the vegetables their customers requested. They partnered with local farmers to grow the rest. Now the Birri Brothers are Montreal's most-respected purveyors of fresh, local vegetables. They sell only what is in season and what grows here. No pineapples or avocados.

This is where Montrealers come to learn how to grow a fig tree, make a *giardiniera* or stuff zucchini blossoms. It's where you buy parsley and basil plants for your garden in the spring or 20 bushels of San Marzano tomatoes in August to make the year's supply of pasta sauce. It's also the place to rub shoulders with the city's hottest chefs. There is Martin Picard in oversized sunglasses buying hot peppers for Au Pied de Cochon. Normand Laprise has just passed through, seeing what's new. Éric Girard is hand-picking nasturtium flowers for his hip Old Montreal bakery, Olive & Gourmando.

"It's about trust," Lino Birri says. "Whether you are buying a single plant or 12 cases of vegetables, we give everyone the same attention. And you always know what you're getting."

Lino & Bruno, the Pirri Brothers

Birri Brothers lunch

"Hi Ma, I'm hungry. What are you cooking?" That's Tony Passarelli on the phone to his mother. Tony is a longtime worker at the Birri Brothers stall. His mother lives in Little Italy, two blocks from the market. A little later, like magic, Mama appears with a serving of penne and homemade tomato sauce with meatballs. Lunchtime at the Birri Brothers market stall and everyone, it seems, is eating like a Roman. Mama Birri sometimes sends pizza. The Baldassarre brothers, Mario, Joe and Frank, all have hot lunches, too, courtesy of their mother. If it's Thursday, lunch will be a veritable feast – or as their boss, Lino Birri, calls it, "the Baldassarre buffet." That's because Wednesday nights, the whole Baldassarre clan gathers at their parents' house for supper. And there are always plenty of leftovers: grilled chicken and lamb, eggplant parmigiana, lasagna. Each son gets an army-size care package to heat up for lunch at the market the next day, enough for everybody to dig into.

"It's a nice chance to relax, in the peace and quiet back here," says Joe Baldassarre, hidden away at the back of the stall with the rib steak he has just sliced into a bowl of baby radicchio leaves plucked from a nearby rack. "And Mom's cooking is always delicious."

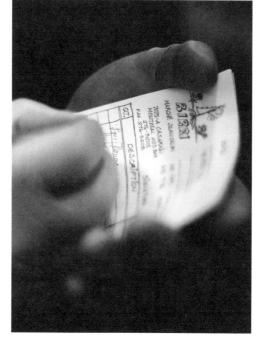

Pull up a chair

You have to be romantic to love fava beans, one of the oldest cultivated plants in the world. Or if not romantic, obsessive. Fresh, local favas appear for a few weeks in early summer, bushels of long, gnarly green fingers awaiting shelling. Getting to the tender, edible beans buried under two layers of pod and skin is archeologist's work. Slit the fur-lined outer green shell with your fingernail and gently squeeze to pop the beans out. Their white coverings will be bitter and tough, requiring further peeling. A pound of whole favas and half an hour's labour yield but a half-cup of beans.

The first favas are small and tender with the feel of butter and the tang of fresh almonds. They are delicious cooked briefly and mashed with olive oil and a little salt.

English-speakers call them broad beans; in French they are *gourganes*; in Arabic, *foul*. But it is Italians who love them most, in soups and stews or sautéed with pancetta and mint. The best way to eat favas, though, is on the porch while shelling them, the way the backyard gardeners in Little Italy do – with a bottle of homemade white wine, a hunk of Romano cheese and a mound of sea salt to dip them in.

Fresh Mozzarella with Zucchini Ribbons

There are waiting lists for the pure-white, buttery burrata that arrives from Puglia in southern Italy every two weeks at Fromagerie Hamel and at Capitole, the market's Italian emporium. Some customers even lay down a deposit to secure a $30 ball of the fresh mozzarella cheese, chewy on the outside and creamy on the inside. Burrata is inimitable, but fresh local mozzarella, also known as *fior di latte*, makes a fine substitute with a considerably smaller carbon footprint.

Burrata is served with ribbons of zucchini in a delicate citrus sauce at Little Italy's Café Via Dante, a few blocks from the market.

(Serves 2)

2 small zucchinis, ends removed

juice of ½ lemon

zest of 1 orange

salt and freshly ground pepper

8 oz (225 g) burrata or fresh mozzarella cheese

extra-virgin olive oil

1 orange, peeled and segmented

Slice zucchinis lengthwise into the thinnest possible ribbons (a mandoline works well). In a shallow, non-reactive bowl or baking dish, marinate zucchini in lemon juice, orange zest, salt and pepper for at least an hour or until softened.

Arrange the zucchini slices on a serving plate. Cut mozzarella in thick slices and arrange over the zucchini. Pour the marinade over the top. Drizzle with olive oil and garnish with orange segments. Serve with fresh crusty bread.

Fiori di zucca

There are those who wait for zucchinis to grow to club-size, for shredding into cakes and muffins. Others prefer them in their infancy, the seed-free miniatures sautéed or steamed.

But those who fall under the spell of the pretty yellow blossoms are willing to forgo all that. Beautiful to behold, *fiori di zucca* (as they are called in Italian) are also edible and absolutely delicious thinly sliced and scattered over pasta or into an omelette. Better still, coat lightly in tempura batter and fry until golden in hot oil.

The star-shaped zucchini flowers are not easy to find, though. They also are highly perishable and wilt miserably if not eaten the day they are picked. Luckily, zucchini flowers arrive every morning throughout the growing season at the Birri Brothers stand.

Tomates Confites

Plum tomatoes have less juice and fewer seeds than other tomatoes. I like roasting them, which concentrates their flavour and brings out a candy-like quality in the juices that accumulate in the pan. They are a beautiful thing straight out of the oven alongside grilled meat or chicken, but equally delicious as a topping for pizza or polenta, or in sandwiches, frittatas, even soups.

(Makes about 8 cups (2 l))
¼ cup (60 ml) olive oil
7 lb (about 3 kg) plum tomatoes, washed, quartered and cored
coarse salt
freshly ground pepper
12 sprigs fresh thyme

Preheat oven to 425°F (220°C).
Pour half the oil into a large roaster or rimmed baking tray. Lay tomato quarters in a single layer. Season with salt and pepper. Pull the thyme leaves off the sprigs and scatter them over the tomatoes. Add remaining oil, tossing to coat the tomatoes. Roast uncovered for 90 minutes on bottom rack of oven, stirring once or twice, until the tomatoes are soft and slightly charred and the juices have mostly evaporated, leaving a richly coloured and deeply flavoured sauce.

The skins peel off easily after roasting, and some people like to remove them. But not everybody minds the extra texture they add. Serve immediately or let cool and store in the refrigerator for up to two weeks, or in the freezer for a month or so.

Tomatomania

The market is under siege, and the stalls have been commandeered. Everywhere, tomatoes have landed. Meaty beefsteaks for slicing; Italian plums for cooking; candy-sweet cherry tomatoes in a rainbow of colours; and weird-shaped heirlooms with the craziest names: Black Russian, Cherokee Purple, Green Zebra, Amazon Chocolate. Mr. Stripey?

Nothing tastes better than the tomatoes of summer. An old cliché, but it's true. Imported tomatoes, the ones we eat all winter, are flawlessly round and uniformly red, but their beauty, alas, is only skin deep. Field tomatoes are something else altogether, imperfectly perfect. They are furrowed, cracked and dimpled, with the scent of grass and grapefruit. Their lines and dots document the weather: healed-over cracks if it's been a rainy summer and brown spots if it has been cold. Cut one open, and the fruit of the field tomato shines like jelly and bursts with small, slippery seeds. Its taste is sharp and sweet all in the same bite.

Little Italy BLT

This rendition of a summer icon pays homage to Little Italy and the bakers, grocers and vegetable sellers who give Jean Talon Market its Italian flair. It packs spicy pancetta, arugula and pesto into an olive ciabatta roll. And, of course, inch-thick slices of the fattest, juiciest tomatoes.

(Makes 4 sandwiches)
8 slices rolled pancetta
4 olive ciabatta rolls
mayonnaise
4 slices strong provolone cheese
¾ cup (180 ml) roasted red peppers slices
2 large ripe tomatoes, thickly sliced
handful of arugula leaves
basil pesto (see recipe)

Heat a frying pan and cook pancetta slices until lightly browned and crisp. Drain on paper towel.

Slice ciabatta buns in half. Dress bottom halves with mayonnaise, two slices of pancetta, a slice of provolone, red pepper and a slice of tomato. Top with a few arugula leaves. Spread top half of bun with a spoonful of pesto. Close sandwich.

Serve with Brio soft drink or bitters.

Basil Pesto

(Makes 1 cup (250 ml))
2 cups (500 ml) loosely packed basil leaves
2 cloves garlic, peeled and chopped
pinch of coarse salt
¼ cup (60 ml) pine nuts, toasted
½ cup (125 ml) extra-virgin olive oil
¼ cup (60 ml) grated Parmesan cheese

Wash and dry basil, remove stems. Using a mortar and pestle or in a food processor, crush basil leaves, garlic, salt and pine nuts to a paste. Add olive oil in a thin, steady stream, mixing continuously, to make a thick, creamy sauce. Stir in Parmesan. Taste and adjust salt, if necessary.

Use immediately or store in an airtight jar in the refrigerator for several days or in the freezer for up to six months. (Omit cheese if storing for later use.)

Corn Fritters

Nothing beats buttered corn on the cob, polished off the day it was picked. But there is only so much corn on the cob a person can eat. Crisp, spicy corn fritters make good use of the rest. Vegetarians can omit the bacon.

(Serves 6 to 8 as an appetizer)
½ lb (250 g) bacon, chopped
1 cup (250 ml) cooked corn kernels
1 egg
1 cup (250 ml) milk
1 tsp baking powder
½ tsp salt
2/3 cup (160 ml) flour
1 shallot, minced
1 tsp hot smoked paprika
1 tsp ground cumin
1 tsp hot sauce
2 tbsp chopped fresh coriander
vegetable oil for frying

Fry bacon until crisp. Remove from heat and drain on paper towel.

In a large mixing bowl with electric beater, beat egg and milk. In a small bowl, sift together baking powder, salt and flour. Add to egg mixture, stirring just until combined. Fold in fried bacon, corn, shallot, seasonings and chopped coriander.

In a heavy skillet, heat ½ inch (1 cm) oil over medium-high heat until hot but not smoking. Drop in spoonfuls of batter, being careful not to overcrowd the pan. Fry fritters until bottoms are golden, no more than a minute. Flip and fry until the other sides are golden. Transfer to paper towel to drain. Keep warm in low oven. Continue cooking until all fritters are fried. Serve with chipotle crema (see recipe).

Chipotle Crema

1 cup (250 ml) sour cream
1 tsp mayonnaise
1 tsp chopped chipotle peppers in adobo sauce
1 tsp freshly squeezed lime juice

Combine all ingredients and taste. Add extra chipotle peppers for a spicier sauce. Refrigerate until serving time.

Blueberry Pavlova

A pillow of meringue, crispy outside and soft and chewy inside, is spread with whipped cream and heaped with fresh summer berries. That is the dessert created by a New Zealand chef for Russian prima ballerina Anna Pavlova in the 1920s.

(Serves 8 to 10)
For meringue:

6 egg whites, at room temperature
1 tsp cream of tartar
¼ tsp salt
1½ cups (375 ml) sugar

For topping:

1 cup (250 ml) whipping cream, cold
1 tbsp sugar
2 cups (500 ml) blueberries

Preheat oven to 225°F (105°C).

For the meringue: Using a dinner plate as a guide, draw a 9-inch (23 cm) circle in the centre of a sheet of parchment paper. Flip the sheet so the pencil line is facing downward. Lay it on an ungreased baking sheet.

Using an elecric mixer, beat egg whites, cream of tartar and salt on medium-low speed. Beat about 5 minutes or until soft peaks form. Raise speed to medium-high and add sugar 1 tbsp at a time. Raise speed to high and beat 5 more minutes until the meringue is very stiff and glossy.

With a rubber spatula, spread the meringue onto the parchment-covered baking sheet, using the circle as a guide. Mound the outside of the circle slightly higher than the centre.

Bake on low rack of oven for 45 minutes or until meringue is very lightly coloured and slightly crisp to the touch. Remove from oven and let stand at room temperature until completely cooled. Carefully peel away parchment paper and transfer meringue to a serving plate.

For the topping : In a medium bowl, beat whipping cream until soft peaks form. Add sugar and continue beating until stiff peaks form. Spread meringue with whipped cream, top with berries.

 Meringue

- - -

The most important things to remember when making meringue: Have egg whites at room temperature, without even a trace of egg yolk; beat them in a stainless steel or copper bowl at gradually increasing speed; and make sure bowl and attachments are completely grease-free.

Late Summer Plum Cake

Here is an heirloom Ukrainian plum cake that makes good use of the plump, purple-blue plums that come to market in late summer.

(Serves 8 to 10)

For cake:

½ cup (125 ml) butter, softened

¾ cup (180 ml) sugar

2 eggs

1 tsp vanilla

1½ cups (375 ml) flour

1 tsp baking powder

¼ tsp salt

½ cup (125 ml) milk

12 medium plums, pitted and sliced but not peeled

For topping:

½ cup (125 ml) packed brown sugar

2 tbsp flour

1 tsp cinnamon

¼ cup (60 ml) butter, cold

Preheat oven to 350°F (180°C).
Grease a 9-inch (2.5 l) springform pan.

Prepare cake: In a large mixing bowl, cream butter and sugar with an electric mixer until fluffy. Beat in eggs, one at a time, until blended. Add vanilla.

In a separate bowl, sift together flour, baking powder and salt. Add this to butter mixture, alternating with milk, beating at low speed until just combined. Spoon batter into prepared pan, spreading to smooth top. Lay plum slices in a single layer over the top.

Prepare topping: In a small bowl, combine sugar, flour and cinnamon. Using a fork or pastry blender, cut in butter in small pieces until mixture resembles coarse meal. Sprinkle topping over plums.

Bake 35 minutes or until a wooden skewer inserted into centre of cake comes out dry.

Let cake cool 10 to 15 minutes before removing sides of pan.

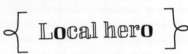

{ Local hero }

The Mont Royal plum is a true Montrealer. A tough little tree, it withstands long, brutish winters and blooms early every spring. Baskets of inky-blue Mont Royal plums appear at the market in mid-September. There are other plums, too, but they grow in more temperate zones. Only the Mont Royal is hardy enough to grow here. The skin of the medium-size, round fruit is almost black and its yellow flesh is soft, juicy and amazingly sweet. Mont Royals are perfect for eating, but equally divine for baking and preserving.

Prunus domestica "Mont Royal" was developed in William Dunlop's orchard in Outremont, on the slopes of Mount Royal, in 1892. He presented his self-pollinating, European-style plum tree to the Quebec Pomological Society in 1902 and it became an overnight sensation, soon planted by orchard keepers around the city. More than a century later, this heirloom Montreal plum remains a late-summer favourite at the market.

· THE BEEKEEPER ·

Stephen Matthews

Bees, like humans, prefer blue skies. But yesterday, a flash storm blew in before Stephen Matthews could get all his honey off the hives. The bees, feeling ornery, stung him no fewer than 60 times. The karma is different in the bee yard today. The late afternoon sun dips behind the apple trees as the beekeeper arrives. Just a quick puff from his smoker and the females are mollified (the males never sting). They buzz languorously around his head — alighting on his face, his arms, his chest — then fly off again without malice. This is one of a dozen orchards and pastures in the western Laurentians, near Lachute, where Matthews stations his 400 hives and their two million resident honeybees.

Leaning on a beehive, joking and chatting, Matthews seems oblivious to the hum, even without protective netting. The beekeeper avoids cologne, aftershave and shiny jewelry, which he knows will pique the bees' curiosity. He wears light-coloured clothes because dark ones rile them. When it is rainy, or hot and muggy, he steers clear; the bees will be agitated. Once, when he was a teenager, Matthews stopped breathing and lost consciousness after being stung. At the hospital, he was diagnosed with a severe allergy to bee venom. So he carried around a syringe of epinephrine, then quit the business altogether, leaving the beehives to his father. But he never shed his fascination for honeybees. Eventually, he had himself tested again and found he had outgrown the allergy.

North American bees have been in decline for decades, victims of mites, fungus and pesticides. Their numbers today are half what they were 60 years ago. Still, these tenacious creatures keep at it. The field bees travel up to three kilometres at a time, 40 trips a day, in search of nectar and pollen to bring back to their queen. In a lifetime, each will produce 1/12th of a teaspoon of honey. It is the equivalent of flying 3½ times the earth's circumference for a pound of honey.

Matthews hauls the honey-filled trays back to the honey house, where the honey is extracted from the wax, then filtered and jarred. His clover honey is mild and pale, with hints of vanilla, a synthesis of the bees' late-summer sojourns in fields ablaze with goldenrod and wild aster. The buckwheat honey is bold and piquant, dark amber in colour. Sunshine in a jar.

Stephen, St-André-d'Argenteuil

Melon music

Thump, thump. That's how to choose the perfect watermelon. Buying the ripest, juiciest one isn't easy. A watermelon's thick, hard rind conceals what is happening inside. Vegetable farmer Liette Lauzon reaches into a crate of green-striped behemoths and hoists out the heaviest one. She holds it to her ear and gives a series of taps with the palm of her hand, listening for a clear, hollow "tonk." Some people look to the yellow underbelly of the watermelon, where it lay in the field, as an indicator of ripeness. (If the spot is white the melon isn't ready, the theory goes.) Others gauge the glossiness of the rind: not too bright and not too dull. Weight is important, too, since a watermelon is more than 90 per cent water. A heavy melon is at peak maturity.

But Lauzon, who has been growing and selling them for decades, says the surest way to choose a watermelon is to listen to its music.

Disappearing bees

Dinner would be pretty meagre without bees. There would be no meat, no vegetables. No flowers on the table. No apple pie or wine either.

Bees produce honey, but they play a much more important role as agricultural pollinators. They are behind one out of every three bites we take, pollinating everything from soybeans and blueberries to cucumbers, broccoli and clover for animal feed.

But they are in crisis. Bee populations around the world have dropped by as much as 50 to 75 per cent over the last couple of decades in a mysterious phenomenon known as colony collapse disorder. The usual suspects appear on the list of probable causes: increased pesticide use, global warming, habitat destruction. But scientists say it could be mites, insect diseases, malnutrition, even stress.

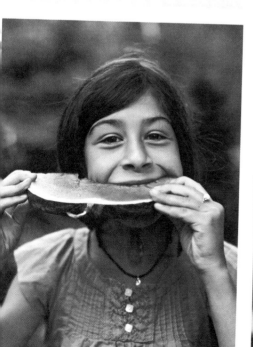

· THE CARNIVORES' CONFIDANT ·

Patrick Loyau

He knows who is divorced, who is on a diet. Who has been fired, or promoted. What the kids are up to and when the in-laws are coming. Who can cook and who can't. Patrick Loyau hears all manner of confession and admission from behind the meat counter at La Boucherie du Marché. It's an old-fashioned shop on the southern perimeter of the market, where carnivores come once or twice a week for their pork chops and rib steaks, their ham-and-mustard-stuffed chicken *crapaudine* and pheasant *ballotines*.

Loyau knows his regulars by name, marbling preference and dietary habits. He knows who's too busy to marinate their own flank steak, who has picky eaters for friends or is trying desperately to impress a new lover. "I'm like a hairdresser," Loyau says with a conspiratorial grin. "My customers tell me everything. Well, almost everything."

Loyau says a good butcher doesn't just carve hulking sides of beef into artful cuts of filet mignon, *onglet* and sirloin. He's got to be a good listener, and a storyteller, too. His father and uncles – who learned to be butchers in Loire, France – taught him that. So did the old-timers he recruited when he opened his shop. In an era of anonymous supermarkets and Styrofoam packaging, Loyau's customers are hungry for information about their meat: who raised it, what the animal ate and how to cook it. He seeks out local producers of conventional and specialty meats. He prefers family-run farms that slaughter fewer than 25 lambs a week, whose guinea fowls peck for bugs and grasses in open-air aviaries all summer, whose boar forage for acorns and berries in woods and fields.

A cook himself, Loyau shares recipes for carbonnade, *pot au feu* and *magret de canard*. And just like the fruit and vegetable stalls, Loyau's meat counters change with the season. In summer, there are mounds of sausages – 26 kinds, the specialty of the house, made fresh daily – and marinated pork and chicken brochettes for the barbecue. When autumn arrives, he offers rabbit stuffed with prunes and herbs, as well as beef brisket and pork shoulder for braising and stewing. Just in time for Christmas, there will be terrines studded with fruit and nuts, plus goose and turkey ready for stuffing.

La Boucherie du Marché Patrice

Lamb Kebabs

On Sunday afternoons, families gather on Mount Royal, lingering until sunset. They spread out endless banquets on the picnic tables and grill *köfte* and kebabs like these on their portable metal grills.

Kebabs are best cooked by direct grilling over high heat on a charcoal or gas grill. The high heat sears the meat and seals in the juices. Before grilling, remove excess fat from the meat to minimize flare-ups. One inch is the optimal size for the meat cubes to ensure even cooking. Metal skewers are best, but use oven mitts when handling them. Wooden skewers work, too, but need to be soaked to prevent them from burning.

(Makes 12 skewers)
For marinade:

1 small onion, grated

5 cloves garlic, crushed

½ cup (125 ml) olive oil

¼ cup (60 ml) white wine

¼ cup (60 ml) freshly squeezed lemon juice

3 tbsp finely chopped fresh rosemary

1 tbsp dried mint

1 tsp salt

1 tsp freshly ground pepper

1 tsp dried oregano

2½-lb (1 kg) boneless leg of lamb, cut into 1-inch (2.5 cm) cubes

2 red onions, cut into wedges

pita bread, for serving

lemon wedges, for serving

Combine marinade ingredients. In a large, shallow non-reactive bowl or baking dish, toss lamb cubes with marinade, mixing well to coat the meat. Cover and refrigerate for at least 8 hours or overnight.

Half an hour before ready to grill, remove meat from fridge and let come to room temperature. Drain lamb cubes, reserving marinade. Thread onto skewers, 5 or 6 cubes per skewer, alternating with onion wedges.

In a small saucepan over medium-high heat, bring reserved marinade to a boil and simmer 5 minutes. Set aside.

Oil the grill grate and preheat to high. Grill kebabs, turning frequently with tongs and basting with marinade, 8 to 10 minutes or until lamb is nicely browned and onion is charred. Using tongs or an oven mitt, transfer kebabs to a large platter lined with pita bread. Garnish with lemon wedges and serve with tzatziki (see recipe).

Tzatziki

2 medium cucumbers

¼ tsp salt

2 cups (500 ml) thick Greek-style yogurt

2 tsp lemon juice

1 clove garlic, minced

¼ cup (60 ml) finely chopped fresh dill

¼ cup (60 ml) chopped fresh mint

1 tbsp extra-virgin olive oil

Peel, seed and coarsely grate cucumbers. In a large sieve over a bowl, sprinkle grated cucumber with salt and let stand 10 minutes. Squeeze out excess liquid. Add salted cucumber to remaining ingredients and mix well. Taste and adjust seasoning if desired. Keep refrigerated until ready to use.

Portuguese Piri Piri Chicken

South of the market, around St. Laurent Blvd. and Rachel St., the Portuguese rotisseries send up plumes of smoke when their spicy chicken goes on to grill. It makes everybody's mouth water. At home, piri piri chicken can be cooked on a ridged stovetop grill pan or a gas barbecue. If you can, opt for a charcoal barbecue for a deeper, smokier flavour.

(Serves 3 to 4)
For marinade:

freshly squeezed juice of 1 lemon (about ¼ cup/60 ml)

1/3 cup (80 ml) olive oil

3 tbsp hot pepper paste

4 cloves garlic, minced

1 tsp dried oregano

1 tbsp smoked sweet paprika

½ cup (125 ml) chopped fresh parsley

2 bay leaves, crumbled

1 tsp salt

1 4-lb (2 kg) chicken, butterflied*

lemon wedges, for garnish

In a small bowl, combine marinade ingredients. Pour half the marinade into a large, shallow, non-reactive bowl or baking dish. Reserve the rest of the mixture to serve with the grilled chicken. Add chicken to the marinade and toss to coat well. Use your hands to massage the marinade under the chicken skin and into the meat. Cover and refrigerate at least 8 hours or overnight. When ready to cook, remove chicken from marinade and drain.

Prepare the grill, oiling the grill grate. When grill is hot, cook chicken skin-side up over high heat, basting often, for about 5 minutes, moving the chicken around on the grill to prevent flare-ups. Flip, baste and continue cooking another 5 minutes. Move chicken away from the hot coals to cook over indirect heat, basting regularly, for another 20 minutes or until well browned and cooked through. The internal temperature of the thickest part of the thigh should be 165°F to 170°F (74°C to 76°C). Transfer chicken to a serving platter, cut into pieces and garnish with lemon wedges. Serve with the reserved piri piri sauce.

* To butterfly a chicken, place the whole chicken breast-side down on a cutting board. Cut along each side of the backbone and remove it. Press firmly on the centre of the breast to break the bone and flatten the chicken. (Or ask the butcher to do it.)

Patatas

Bay leaf, oregano and smoked paprika give these potatoes their Portuguese personality. This is the perfect recipe for new potatoes, or *grelots* as we call them in Quebec. These are the tiny summer potatoes harvested before they are mature. The skins are so thin that *grelots* never need peeling.

(Serves 8)
For spice blend:

4 bay leaves, crumbled

½ tsp coarse salt

1 tsp peppercorns

1 tsp dried oregano

1 tbsp smoked sweet paprika

2 lb (1 kg) new potatoes, washed

3 tbsp olive oil

4 cloves garlic, crushed

1 cup (250 ml) finely chopped fresh parsley

½ tsp saffron

1¼ cups (310 ml) water

Grind spices into a powder using a mortar and pestle or a spice grinder. Store in an airtight jar until ready to use.

Place potatoes, olive oil, garlic, parsley, saffron and water in a large, heavy-bottomed saucepan. Cover and bring to a boil over medium-high heat. Lower heat and simmer, uncovered, stirring often, until water has evaporated and potatoes are soft, about 30 minutes. Add a little extra water if necessary to keep the potatoes from sticking.

Remove to a large serving bowl and let cool slightly. Smash potatoes with a wooden spoon or the heel of your hand to break them up. Season with 2 tsp of the spice blend and toss well to coat. Add an extra drizzle of olive oil just before serving. Serve warm or at room temperature.

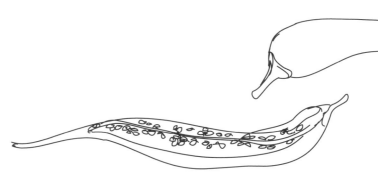

· THE GARLIC CHAMPION ·

Daniel Brais

"Chinese garlic." Daniel Brais practically spits the words. China is the world's largest garlic producer, growing three-quarters of the global supply. Those ubiquitous mesh bags of Chinese bulbs that sell for a dollar are what most people buy. But from his stand at Jean Talon Market, Brais is waging a David and Goliath battle to change that – one hairy-rooted head of local garlic at a time. On a breezy afternoon at the height of garlic season, Brais wolfs down his ham sandwich and jumps up to answer a customer's question, explaining with unflagging enthusiasm how his garlic grows. He flips open his pocket knife and slices a fat, juicy clove for customers to smell. His recipe for roasted garlic with new potatoes and thyme makes their mouths water.

Brais, who grows six varieties of softneck garlic and a small assortment of other vegetables on 10 acres of sandy soil at Ferme des Moissons in St-Urbain on Montreal's South Shore, has just completed a month-long marathon. The whole clan pitched in to dig up their garlic by hand so as not to bruise the fresh, new bulbs. For the next three weeks, the garlic lay flat on wooden drying racks to cure in cool, dry storage rooms with the doors open and fans blowing. Brais's mother and his aunt braided the garlic heads together by the stalks, creating decorative plaits.

Many farmers plant their garlic in the fall, but Brais and his father Jean-Guy wait until spring to avoid the tyranny of Quebec's freeze-and-thaw winters. In July, when the leaves wither and the stalks bend, it is time to pry the newly formed bulbs of summer garlic from the soil. A second crop of later garlic will be ready in late August. Timing the harvest is tricky. Pick garlic too soon and the flavours and juices won't have reached their peak. Left too long in the ground, the garlic heads split and the cloves rot. Garlic, Brais will tell you with a pride earned by growing thousands of pounds of it a year, can be a finicky crop.

Daniel, Ferme des Moissons

Roasted Garlic

Roasting garlic smooths its sharp edges. This recipe from the Brais family of garlic growers makes a creamy spread that is delicious on toasted baguette or roasted vegetables, or in soups.

(Makes about ½ cup (125 ml))
4 large heads garlic, whole and unpeeled
2 tbsp olive oil
salt and freshly ground pepper
2 tbsp fresh thyme leaves
2 tsp good-quality balsamic vinegar

Preheat oven to 375°F (190°C).
Slice the top off each head of garlic to expose the cloves inside. Lay garlic heads, cut side up, on a large sheet of aluminum foil. Drizzle 1 tbsp of the olive oil over them and season with salt, pepper and thyme. Fold up foil to form a tightly sealed packet. Roast 60 minutes. Test with a fork; the garlic is done when the cloves are soft and easily pierced. Remove from oven and let cool slightly. Unwrap foil and squeeze the contents of each clove into a small bowl. Mash the roasted garlic with balsamic vinegar and the remaining 1 tbsp of olive oil. Taste and adjust seasonings if necessary. Serve warm.

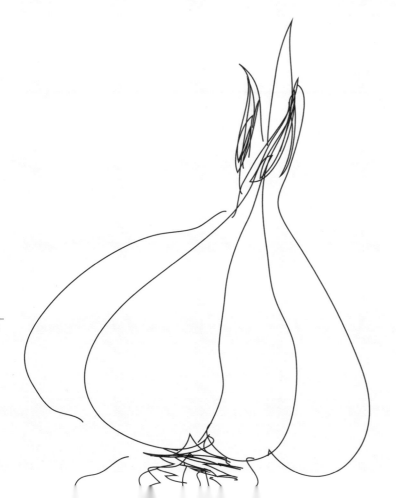

Softneck or hardneck?

Garlic is garlic, the uninitiated might say. But garlic has an extensive family tree. There are more than a hundred strains, each with its own personality traits and flavour, ranging from mild to spicy. Porcelain garlics are beautiful, with their satiny white wrappers, fat cloves and pronounced flavour. Purple-stripe garlics have elegant-coloured skins and numerous slender cloves. Rocamboles have reddish wraps and loose inner skins. Whatever the cultivar, all garlic falls into one of two subspecies: softneck or hardneck. Softneck garlic (*Allium sativum, var. sativum*) is the garlic you see at the market, braided and hung for display. Once dried, it keeps well over longer periods. It gets its name from the plant's stalk, which becomes soft and pliable at maturity.

Hardneck garlic (*Allium sativum, var. ophioscorodon*) has a long, rigid stalk that grows right up from inside the bulb. It has fewer, but larger, cloves. Garlic is often planted in the fall, and some say hardneck is better suited to northern climates. As a bonus, hardneck garlic produces beautiful coiling scapes in May and June that are prized by cooks for their bright-green colour and subtle garlicky flavour.

Both types of garlic should be stored in a cool, dry place away from heat and sunlight and protected from fluctuations in temperature.

PATATES
À CHAIR
JAUNES
FRANCELINE

Pied
Bleu
7.00/
100g

3/2.00

5/2.00

- FALL -

(Harvest)

....

Almost without warning, summer slips into fall. Leaves turn, days shorten and the market's palette shifts to amber and ochre, russet and burgundy.

With one more flurry of activity the farmers rescue the last of their summer crops from late September's killing frosts, which can wither a field of tomatoes or basil in a single overnight swoop. As they leave for the day, vendors throw blankets over their stalls, as if tucking their babies into bed for the night.

By October, the growing season is all but over, except for the hardiest cabbages, the late root vegetables still sizing up in the ground, and Cortland apples, whose sweetness is heightened by a brush with the cold. Still, there is plenty to celebrate at Jean Talon Market. This is the time for apples and pears, for carrots and parsnips. It's the season for weird winter squashes sporting turbans and tails, spots and stripes. For Romanesco cauliflower with prehistoric spikes, dusty purple cabbage as big as Jupiter, and stalks of Brussels sprouts like bumps on a log.

There is a tinge of melancholy as the walls go up in late October and the whole place retracts like a snail into its shell. The market is just a wisp of what it was a few weeks ago. Everyone is tired, longing for home after summer's marathon, and a little mournful, too. By November, the wind blows damp and cold and many of the stands stay covered in plastic, their minders appearing only on weekends to liquidate the last of the late-season bounty.

Still, a sunny, late-fall afternoon at the market — the trees along Mozart Ave. glowing 22-karat gold — can make your heart skip a beat. Ruby-red cranberries from St-Louis-de-Blandford piled high in their bushels sparkle like crown jewels at the museum. Autumn's swan song.

Then a chill creeps up your back and the glow is gone. By 3 p.m., the sun has slunk down in an aluminum-grey sky. Jacques Rémillard's nose drips and his hands are cold and red as he loads his unsold parsnips and parsley roots into the back of the truck before heading home. All anybody wants is to be inside.

It's getting chilly. Time for soup, stew and apple crisp.

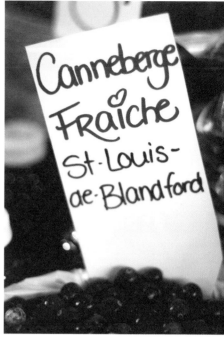

Canneberge
Fraîche ♡
St·Louis-
de·Blandford

Courge
Spaguetti
2.⁰⁰

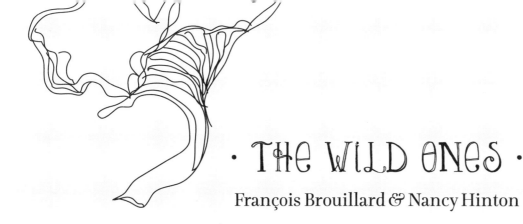

· THE WILD ONES ·

François Brouillard & Nancy Hinton

She was a pretty young chef from Ste-Adèle. He was a rugged forager from St-Roch-de-l'Achigan. Nancy Hinton was working overtime to prove herself in the kitchen at L'Eau à la bouche, one of Quebec's most illustrious restaurants. François Brouillard was eking out a living doing what he loved best: rambling through fields and forests in search of wild food, sleeping in a trailer, chasing the seasons. He turned up at the restaurant's back door every Thursday, selling knobs of wild ginger, a fistful of sea spinach or baskets of the first fiddleheads or morels, the same wild treasures that fill his stall at the market. "He would show up, tanned and rugged, with all these interesting ingredients I had never even heard of before," recalls Hinton, pulling a pine needle from her sweetheart's hair as she talks. It is a sunny mid-October morning, and she has laid out the autumn mushrooms that Brouillard and his freelance foragers have just brought in. "And he smelled of fresh air."

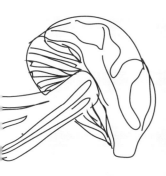

It was the fungi that won her over, though. "To court me, he would leave bags of wild mushrooms at my doorstep. I'd get home after work – and there would be a few rare lobster mushrooms," Hinton recalls, her petite face lighting up with the memory. Sometimes there would be a bouquet of wild flowers, too. One day a bag of boletes turned up at her door, and she called to thank Brouillard. But they hadn't come from him.

"Who else is leaving you mushrooms?" he quizzed her. "What kind of mushrooms? Anything special?" It was a secret admirer, it turned out, another chef at the restaurant. But by then the new suitor didn't stand a chance. Hinton was smitten with Brouillard. He and his wild things had cast their spell.

Soon, she was spending her days off cooking at À la Table des jardins sauvages, his rustic restaurant in St-Roch-de-l'Achigan, an hour's drive northeast of Montreal, not far from Joliette. Now they live together, the forager and the chef, in a cottage near the restaurant. There, she experiments with mushroom caramel candies and cattail broth in a kitchen lined with jars of mocha- and chocolate-scented dried mushrooms. And he still roams the woods.

Les Jardins Sauvages

François & Nancy

Wild Mushroom & Venison Tartare

This tartare from chef Nancy Hinton uses wild mushrooms, like porcini and chanterelles, and cultivated shiitakes and oysters. Though the venison is raw, wild mushrooms must always be cooked before eating.

(*Serves 4 as an appetizer*)

½ lb (250 g) fresh mushrooms, brushed clean and diced

4 tbsp extra-virgin olive oil

¾-lb (350 g) fillet of venison, beef or bison

2 small shallots, minced

2 tbsp Dijon mustard

2 tbsp finely chopped fresh chives

1 tbsp finely chopped fresh parsley

½ tsp lemon juice, freshly squeezed

salt and freshly ground pepper

multigrain crackers

fresh thyme, for garnish

Sauté mushrooms in 2 tbsp of the oil over medium-high heat until lightly browned, about 10 minutes. Allow to cool. Just before serving, chop the raw meat: With a sharp knife, cut the fillet into thin slices, then chop finely. Add mushrooms to meat, then shallots, mustard, remaining oil, herbs and lemon juice. Stir to combine. Season to taste with salt and pepper. Spoon onto crackers and garnish with thyme. Serve immediately.

Of porcini and puffballs

- - -

To those accustomed to bland button mushrooms, pre-sliced and plastic-wrapped, the wild specimens at François Brouillard's stand at Jean Talon Market come as a shock: crimson lobster mushrooms, fluted gold chanterelles, purple porcini and lacy black trumpets. It's a circus of colours and shapes. Quebec is wild-mushroom nirvana. More than 3,000 species have been identified, growing on decaying tree stumps and high up on maple branches, in mixed and coniferous forests, on suburban lawns and in cow pastures – anywhere the soil is warm and moist enough.

Brouillard's army of 75 or more pickers comb the province from April through October for edible mushrooms with fanciful names like shaggy mane, swollen-stalked cat, hen of the woods and hedgehog. At the height of the season he himself is out from dawn to dusk. On a very good day he will return with $2,000 worth. Head out with him and you will see: Brouillard is obsessed. Head hunched, he watches for telltale signs on the forest floor. Matsutakes grow at the base of conifers; chanterelles in mixed forest near running water. Black trumpets hide in patches of moss. Driving along the highway, "François des bois" (as they call him) veers wildly and U-turns onto the shoulder, clambering into the ditch after a stand of puffballs. Once, when he spotted a circle of fairy ring mushrooms growing in a cemetery, he feigned a graveside prayer, then pulled out his penknife.

· THE TRANSCENDENTALIST ·

Daniel Oligny

There are rows and rows more potatoes to dig up, but the weatherman is threatening torrential rain, which will turn the fields to mud. Still, Daniel Oligny smiles that trademark smile of his. "*Pas de problème*" is his mantra.

This is the last of the season's harvest: thousands of pounds of white potatoes, red potatoes, russets, Charlottes, Rattes and Yukon Golds. Not a bad yield despite incessant June rain that mildewed and destroyed seven acres of potato plants. Oligny never seems to get stressed. Maybe it's the Hindu meditational chants he listens to. Or the fact that his soul is rooted here.

As he manoeuvres the Chevrolet Cheyenne along a rutted road, Oligny time-travels back to his childhood in this very dirt. "My father didn't have much time for us when we were children. He would be out in the fields all day long," Oligny recalled. But a little boy who squeezed himself into the cab of the tractor would be permitted to sit there beside his dad for hours and hours. "He didn't talk much. But I could be with him and watch him work. I loved it."

Oligny Sr. let his son take over the farm, upgrading equipment and acquiring more land in this patchwork quilt of black fields in St-Rémi on Montreal's South Shore. For a long time he grew a dozen different crops, which he sold wholesale. But he has since scaled down. Now he sticks to potatoes and small quantities of peppers and eggplant, selling them at the market and a few grocery stores near home.

Just after 4 p.m. the November sky darkens. Oligny hoists himself back into the tractor and heads for the barn, where crates of potatoes wait to be washed and sorted. But there is nobody squeezed into the cab next to him. Daniel, it seems, is the last of the Oligny family farmers. His son is making a name for himself as a videographer. His daughter wants to be a dancer. "Everybody finds their own happiness," he shrugs.

Daniel, au marché

Blue Chips

Fresh homemade potato chips are delicious served warm and sprinkled with salt, herbs or spice. Blue potatoes are the most fun, and they don't need to be peeled. Or try a combination of different potatoes and other root vegetables.

(Makes 1 medium-size serving bowl)
6 blue potatoes
vegetable oil for frying
coarse sea salt
1 tbsp finely chopped fresh rosemary

Scrub potatoes under running water with a vegetable brush and pat dry. Slice into very thin circles no more than 1/8 inch (3 mm) thick. (A mandoline works best, but watch your fingers.) Soak slices in a bowl of cold water for 30 minutes to release excess starch. Rinse and drain. Dry thoroughly in a clean dishcloth.

Meanwhile, heat about 2 inches (5 cm) of oil to 375°F (190°C) in a deep fryer or deep saucepan. (You'll know the oil is hot enough if the chips begin to sizzle immediately when they are dropped into the oil. It is too hot if they brown instantly.)

Carefully drop the potato slices one by one into the hot oil; work in batches, being careful not to overcrowd the pan. Fry briefly until golden, then remove using a slotted spoon or tongs. Lay the chips out in a single layer on paper towel to drain, salt lightly and sprinkle with rosemary. Let sit for a minute to crisp. Serve warm.

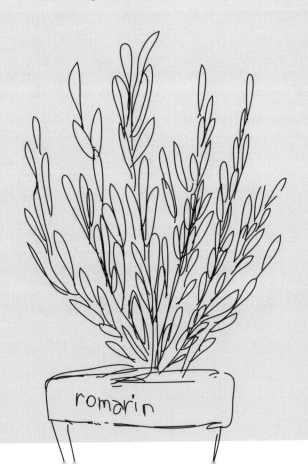

romarin

· THE MIGRANT WORKER ·

Julio Velazquez Cortes

By this time tomorrow, Julio Velazquez Cortes will be home in Tlaxcala, Mexico. It will be hot and sunny, and his wife's spicy *chile rojo* will be bubbling on the kitchen stove in preparation for his homecoming fiesta. Right now, though, Cortes's toes are numb with cold in the damp warehouse where the last of the potatoes dug from the fields must be washed and sorted. It is November 6, his last day on the farm in St-Rémi where he has worked six days a week since the seventh of May, tending pepper seedlings in the greenhouse, planting potatoes, hauling eggplants to market.

Already, his mind is back in Mexico. He has packed his bags with gifts of makeup and perfume for his wife, Ana Maria, and watches, school supplies, jeans and T-shirts for his teenage children, Julio and Estefania.

The North American Free Trade Agreement put many small farms in Mexico out of business, sending *campesinos* like Cortes north in search of work. Back home, the average daily wage is about $7. Here, the 6,000 mostly Mexican and Guatemalan seasonal workers who fill the labour shortage on Quebec farms make 10 times that. But it is lonely, arduous work. And there are plenty of stories of mistreated workers denied medical care or deported to Mexico if they complain about the working conditions.

Cortes isn't so badly off. His boss treats him well, and the trailer where he sleeps is decent. The hardest part is being away from his family and the easygoing rhythm of life in Mexico. To ease their homesickness, the Mexican workers in this rural region south of Montreal organize Sunday soccer games in a nearby park. Food sellers drive over from the city, serving up *churros, tamales* or *chicharonnes* from the back of their trucks.

Cortes sends snapshots of all this home, but no one else in his family has ever left Mexico. They can only imagine his life here. Back in Tlaxcala, though, there is real proof of his summers in St-Rémi – eight so far – and the remittances he sends home. Unlike most of their neighbours, the Corteses own a car and a television. Julio bought his son a computer recently. And he has saved enough to replace the corrugated tin and cardboard atop their house with a real roof, and the dirt floor with concrete. That is why he will be back next spring.

Julio, St-Rémi

| Fall at the market

· THE GO-GETTER ·

Liette Lauzon

Liette Lauzon isn't in cold-weather mode yet. When she got up in the dark this morning, she slipped on her running shoes. She should have worn boots, or at least a pair of woolly socks. There was frost last night, and the day never warmed up. Now, her feet are frozen and she can see her breath in puffy clouds as she moves cabbage crates, jogs in place, sweeps the concrete floor of her stall. Anything to keep warm.

It has been a long season, and lesser mortals would be flagging by now. But not Liette or her husband Jean-Claude, who work a 70-acre fruit and vegetable farm in St-Eustache, northwest of Montreal, with the help of their son Julien, daughters Amélie and Virginie, son-in-law Maxime and Jean-Claude's Uncle Normand, plus seven hired workers.

Jean-Claude has been going non-stop since the beginning of May — in the fields or behind the wheel of his delivery truck. He sneaks a three- or four-hour afternoon nap in his reclining armchair in lieu of a night's sleep. Liette went into high gear in the middle of February, planting seeds in her 10 greenhouses for the hundred different fruits, vegetables and herbs the family sells at their corner kiosk. Since the start of summer, she has been up and out of the house by 4:30 a.m., six days a week.

With a sunny face and a mound of curly black hair, Liette is the market's unofficial mayor who knows everyone and everything. Her husband is a big bear of a man who prefers to mind his own business. Together they have built a life based on hard work, ambition and family devotion. "Work, work, work. It's all they know. They barely stop to breathe," confides their elder daughter, Virginie, as she dishes out shepherd's pie in her parents' kitchen. It's a rare mid-week lunch when the family is all together. But Liette says she and Jean-Claude, who have been married nearly 30 years, can't imagine any other life. They love the farm. Besides, there are bills to pay. Monthly payments are steep on an $80,000 tractor — and they have eight of them.

By late October, most of the Lauzons' fall harvest is sold and the kiosk is about to come down. Still, there is no time to dawdle. In winter, the Lauzons run a snow-clearing business with 600 customers. "We are not afraid of hard work," Liette says, as if it weren't obvious.

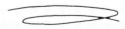

Liette, St-Eustache

Frisée with Bacon & Egg

This robust fall salad – bitter greens and crispy bacon topped with a runny fried egg – is a French bistro classic.

Frisée is that spiky-leafed head of greens also known as curly endive – a profusion of pointy, frizzy leaves around a pale, tender centre. Hardy enough to last in the fields well into November, it has a bitter, almost nutty flavour. This salad also looks fabulous as a mix of bitter greens. Use frisée, Niçoise, escarole, chicory, Belgian endive, even Italian radicchio for a jolt of red.

(Serves 4)
For vinaigrette:
3 tbsp red wine vinegar or apple cider vinegar
freshly ground pepper
2 tbsp finely chopped shallots
1 clove garlic, crushed
6 tbsp extra-virgin olive oil

4 cups (1 l) frisée or other bitter greens, washed and dried
8 oz (225 g) pancetta or thick-cut bacon, cut into cubes or matchsticks
4 large eggs
sea salt and freshly ground pepper

In a medium bowl, whisk together vinegar, pepper, shallots and garlic. Add olive oil in a slow, steady stream, whisking to make a smooth vinaigrette. In a large salad bowl, toss greens with vinaigrette.

Heat a large skillet over medium-high heat. Add bacon and fry for 5 to 10 minutes, stirring, until crispy. Using a slotted spoon, remove to a paper-towel-lined plate. Pour out all but 1 tbsp of the fat and set the skillet aside. Divide greens onto 4 salad plates and sprinkle each with warm bacon.

Heat the skillet again and fry eggs, sunny-side up, for 1 minute or until just set. Slip a fried egg onto each salad. Season with a pinch of sea salt and a liberal grinding of pepper. Serve with slices of toasted baguette.

Roasted Cauliflower Fusilli

This is a Sicilian-inspired pasta, an ode to the giant heads of cauliflower that take over the market in fall with their Gaudi-esque spirals, swirls and spikes. Use the old-fashioned white Snowball variety, spiky green Romanesco, or one of the orange or purple cultivars with names like Violetta, Graffiti, Cheddar and Orange Bouquet. They all taste about the same; the differences are aesthetic. Roasting cauliflower brings out its personality and concentrates its natural sweetness.

(Serves 4)

1 cup (250 ml) raisins

½ tsp saffron

½ cup (125 ml) hot water

1 medium head cauliflower, stems and leaves trimmed, cut into florets

2 large shallots, peeled and sliced

3 tbsp extra-virgin olive oil

coarse salt

freshly ground pepper

1 tbsp finely chopped fresh rosemary

1 lb (500 g) short pasta, such as fusilli or cavatelli

½ cup (125 ml) grated Parmesan cheese

½ tsp crushed dried chili peppers (optional)

Preheat oven to 400°F (200°C).
Combine raisins, saffron and water. Stir and set aside. Place a large pot of salted water on to boil.

Place cauliflower and shallots on a rimmed baking sheet and drizzle with oil, tossing to coat. Season with salt, pepper and rosemary and toss again. Spread vegetables out in a single layer and roast for 20 to 30 minutes, until golden brown.

Halfway through roasting, add pasta to boiling water and cook, uncovered, until al dente, about 10 minutes. Drain.

In a large serving bowl, toss together pasta and roasted vegetables. Add raisins and their soaking liquid, Parmesan cheese and chili peppers. Toss well and serve.

Pumpkin Cinnamon Jelly Roll

(Makes 1 jelly roll)

3 eggs
1 cup (250 ml) brown sugar
¾ cup (180 ml) flour
½ tsp salt
1 tsp baking powder
1 tsp baking soda
1 tsp cinnamon
½ tsp allspice
1 cup (250 ml) puréed pumpkin (fresh or canned)

Filling:

1 cup (250 ml) hazelnuts
1 cup (250 ml) icing sugar
8 oz (225 g) cream cheese, softened
4 tbsp butter, softened
1 tsp vanilla
1 tsp hazelnut liqueur (optional)
icing sugar, for sprinkling

Preheat oven to 375°F (190°C).
Line a 15-by-10-inch (2 l) jelly roll pan with parchment paper and oil lightly.

Beat eggs until frothy, about 5 minutes. Add dry ingredients and beat gently, just until incorporated. Fold in puréed pumpkin. Pour into prepared pan. Bake 15 to 20 minutes or until jelly roll springs back slightly when touched. Leave oven on for hazelnuts.

Lay a clean dishcloth on a counter and carefully flip jelly roll onto it. Slowly peel away parchment paper. While jelly roll is still warm, roll both the jelly roll and the dishcloth lengthwise into a log. Allow to cool.

Meanwhile, prepare the filling: Toast hazelnuts in oven for 10 minutes or until skins blister. Transfer nuts to a dry dish towel and rub gently to remove the skins. Chop the hazelnuts finely in a food processor or with a rolling pin and set aside. Using a hand mixer, combine icing sugar, cream cheese, butter, vanilla and hazelnut liqueur (if using).

Carefully unroll jelly roll onto an oval or rectangular serving platter and remove dishcloth. Spread with filling, then sprinkle evenly with hazelnuts. Re-roll, being careful to keep the roll tight. Sprinkle with icing sugar. Refrigerate until ready to serve, then cut into slices.

{ Pumpkin purée }

The best pumpkins for the kitchen are the so-called pie pumpkins, no bigger than 1½ or 2 kilos. They are sweeter than the big Halloween jack o' lanterns. Cooked and puréed, pumpkin keeps well in the freezer. Its vivid colour and smooth texture make it a major improvement over pumpkin you buy in a can.

To make your own purée, wash the pumpkin in cold water and cut it open with a long, sharp, sturdy knife. Scrape out the seeds and fibres and cut the pumpkin into large chunks. Roast the chunks, skin and all, on a foil-covered baking sheet in a 425°F (220°C) oven until soft enough to pierce with the tip of a knife, about 40 minutes. Alternatively, steam for 15 minutes or until soft.

When cooled, scrape away the skin and purée the pumpkin using a food processor, food mill or potato masher. Use immediately or freeze. A pound (500 g) of whole, unpeeled pumpkin yields about one cup (250 ml) of cooked purée.

Farro & Roasted Butternut Squash

Butternut is a long-keeping winter squash with a sweet, creamy taste and hard, beige skin that is best tackled with a large, sturdy knife or a cleaver. Farro is an ancient form of wheat that Italians have been eating for centuries. Rich in B-complex vitamins and easier to digest than newer forms of wheat, it is gaining newfound popularity everywhere.

Squash and farro make a hearty vegetarian fall or winter supper.

(Serves 6)
2 cups (500 ml) pearled farro
2 tsp salt
6 cups (1.5 l) water
1 medium butternut squash, seeded, peeled and cubed
2 small red onions, thinly sliced
3 tbsp olive oil
½ tsp dried red chili peppers
2 tbsp maple syrup
1 tbsp rice vinegar
2 tsp fresh thyme
salt and freshly ground pepper
½ cup (125 ml) toasted pecans
2 tbsp coarsely chopped fresh parsley

Combine farro, salt and water in a large, heavy saucepan. Bring to a boil over high heat, then reduce to medium-low. Simmer, stirring occasionally to prevent sticking, for 30 minutes. Farro should be tender but al dente. Cook longer if necessary. Remove from heat, drain and set aside. Keep covered.

Preheat oven to 375°F (190°C).
In a large, shallow roasting pan, toss squash and onion with olive oil, chili peppers, maple syrup, rice vinegar, thyme, salt and pepper. Arrange in a single layer and roast in oven for 30 to 40 minutes or until squash is tender.

Spoon farro into a large serving bowl. Top with roasted squash and toss. Scatter with pecans and parsley.

Thai Pumpkin Soup

2 tbsp vegetable oil
2 small onions, chopped
3 cloves garlic, crushed
1 tbsp finely grated fresh ginger
1 tbsp Thai red curry paste
1 small pumpkin peeled, seeded and cubed
1 medium sweet potato, peeled and cubed
1 can (13.5 oz/400 ml) coconut milk
3 cups (750 ml) chicken broth
2 tsp tomato paste
1 tbsp freshly squeezed lime juice

Heat oil in a large saucepan. Sauté onions until translucent. Add garlic, ginger and curry paste and cook briefly, then add remaining ingredients, except lime juice. Bring to a boil, reduce heat and simmer, uncovered, 20 minutes or until pumpkin is tender. Remove from heat and let cool slightly. Transfer to blender and purée until smooth. Add lime juice. Serve garnished with coriander and chili pepper, if desired.

Italian Giardiniera

These spicy vegetables are a staple in Italian households. *Giardiniera* is often included on antipasto plates or served alongside grilled or cured meats.

(Makes 4 x 2-cup (500 ml) jars)

1 head cauliflower, in bite-size florets
6 stalks celery, chopped in ½-inch (1 cm) pieces
6 carrots, chopped in ½-inch (1 cm) rounds
4 red bell peppers, seeded and cut in chunks
1 cup (250 ml) pearl onions, peeled
3 cloves garlic, peeled and thinly sliced
1 cup (250 ml) salt
4 cups (1 l) white vinegar
4 cups (1 l) water
2 tbsp pickling spices
1 tsp ground dried red chili pepper
1 tbsp dried oregano

In a large bowl, toss vegetables with salt. Cover with cold water. Refrigerate several hours or overnight. Drain vegetables and rinse briefly with fresh water. Drain again.

Prepare jars by washing in hot, soapy water and rinsing thoroughly. Make sure lids fit tightly.

In a large pot, heat the vinegar, the 4 cups (1 l) water, pickling spices, dried chili pepper and oregano until boiling. Turn off the heat, add vegetables and stir. Let stand 5 minutes. Pour hot giardiniera into jars, making sure to distribute spices evenly. Also make sure vegetables are completely covered with liquid.

Using a clean, damp cloth, wipe the rims before applying the lids. Let cool slightly, then keep refrigerated. Let marinate at least 2 or 3 days before eating.

Drain before serving.

Japanese Pickled Carrots

This elegant condiment, neither too sharp nor too sweet, pairs nicely with sashimi or steamed fish, but it also stands alone as a salad. An inexpensive hand-held julienne peeler, similar to a potato peeler, turns out long, even strips, but you can also use a sharp knife to cut the carrot into 2- or 3-inch long (5-8 cm) matchsticks.

(Makes 4 x 2-cup (500 ml) jars)

8 cups (2 l) peeled and julienned carrots
2½ cups (625 ml) cider vinegar
2½ cups (625 ml) water
1 cup (250 ml) sugar
1 whole star anise
1-inch (2-3 cm) piece fresh ginger, peeled
2 tsp coarse salt

Soak julienned carrots in a large bowl of cold water for 10 minutes, then drain. Meanwhile, combine vinegar, water, sugar, star anise, ginger and salt in a medium pot. Bring to a boil and reduce heat to low. Simmer for 2 minutes, stirring to dissolve sugar and salt, then remove from heat and cool. In a large pot of boiling water, blanch carrots for 30 seconds. Rinse immediately under cold running water to prevent further cooking. Drain.

Transfer the blanched carrots to clean, dry jars with tight-fitting lids. Pour the pickling vinegar over them, making sure to cover the vegetables with liquid. Clean the jar rims with a clean, damp cloth. Cover tightly. Keep refrigerated. Leave for a day or two for flavours to develop.

Drain before serving.

- Pickled Vegetables, Italian & Asian -

There is a week or two just past the height of summer when the market spills over.
Everything, it seems, has come ripe at the same time. There is too much to eat at
once, so this is the time for freezing and jarring.

On the facing page are two recipes for pickling vegetables – one a spicy Italian
mixed-vegetable *giardiniera* and the other a sweet-and-sour Japanese pickled
carrot. Both will keep their bright colours and crunchy texture for several weeks.
But because they aren't heat-processed after jarring, they need to be refrigerated.

Cortland 10.00

Québec Royal Gala 16.00

Lobo 10.00

McIntosh 6.00

Russet 16.00

St-Eustache SPARTAN 10.00

Délicieuse Rouge Québec 12.00

Empire 10.00

Old-Fashioned Apple Cake

Big, sweet Cortlands are the best apples for baking. They are chopped into this old-fashioned sour-cream coffee cake. It is finished with a streusel topping of nuts and cinnamon. A scoop of vanilla ice cream wouldn't hurt, either.

(Serves 8 to 10)

For cake:

1 cup (250 ml) sour cream

1 tsp baking soda

2 cups (500 ml) sifted flour

2 tsp baking powder

½ tsp salt

½ cup (125 ml) butter, softened

1 cup (250 ml) sugar

4 eggs

1 tsp vanilla

3 cups (750 ml) peeled, chopped apples (3 large apples)

For topping:

¼ cup (60 ml) packed brown sugar

2 tsp cinnamon

2 tbsp finely chopped walnuts

Preheat oven to 350°F (180°C).
Grease and flour an 8-inch square (2 l) or 9-inch round (1.2 l) cake pan.

In a small bowl, combine sour cream and baking soda. Let stand about 10 minutes, until almost double in size. Meanwhile, make topping by combining brown sugar, cinnamon and nuts. Set aside.

In a medium bowl, sift together flour, baking powder and salt. Set aside. In a large mixing bowl using an electric mixer, cream butter and sugar until fluffy, about 5 minutes. Add eggs one at a time, mixing after each addition, and vanilla. Beat well. With mixer on low speed, gradually add flour mixture, alternating with sour-cream mixture, beating just until incorporated. Fold in chopped apples.

Spread half the batter into prepared pan and sprinkle with half the topping. Cover with remaining batter and spread smooth. Sprinkle with remaining topping.

Bake 50 to 60 minutes or until a wooden skewer inserted into the centre comes out clean. Remove cake from oven and let cool 15 minutes before inverting from pan and slicing.

· THE IMPORTER ·

Nino Marcone

Just yesterday, a black limousine pulled up at Chez Nino and the passenger in the back seat rolled down his window. "Are they in yet?" he asked. Nino Marcone slipped into the coldroom at the back of his store and brought out a plastic container of dirt-crusted lumps wrapped in paper towel. When he lifted the cover, the whole place filled with the smell of plowed earth and autumn rain – the unmistakable aroma of truffles. Rare white truffles foraged by a special breed of pigs in the hills of Alba in northern Italy. They are meltingly sublime shaved on pasta or over risotto, and they cost $8,000 a kilogram. "I'll take four," the customer said. Marcone handed them over in a brown paper bag in exchange for $800. "*Buon appetito*," he waved.

Come November, when the outdoor market is reduced to a scattering of tables with a rack or two of Hubbard squash, it is time to step into Marcone's greengrocer – and into the hands of a master importer. Marcone slits open a burlap sack he has just had flown in from Avellino, in the south of Italy. The bag is heavy with burnished brown chestnuts, plump and meaty. It is November 11, the feast of San Martino. Back in Italy, every village is celebrating with roasted chestnuts and a first taste of the *vino novello*, the newly made wine. Marcone himself will take home a bag of the *castagne* tonight and uncork a nice bottle of Brunello di Montalcino to celebrate in absentia.

He went into business in 1967, selling vegetables amid the dealers in live goats, sheep and chickens who kept shop along the market's northern fringe. He was 19 years old and newly arrived from Italy. "With all the animals, the place smelled like hell in summer," he recalled. "But so many of the vendors spoke Italian, and the customers, too. It was as close to home as I could get, so far from Abruzzi."

Over the years, Marcone has built a reputation for his choice offerings and his worldwide connections – for wild arugula from France, white peaches from Pennsylvania, honey-sweet figs from Greece. "Try these. These are the best," Marcone will say, opening his penknife and cutting a wedge for a customer to try. He displays pyramids of white pomegranates from California and ruby-red ones from Spain. The Greek figs are almost finished, but their Brazilian and Argentinian successors will be in soon. The local produce has been upstaging him all summer, but now it is Marcone's time to shine.

Nino, Chez Nino

Chestnut Mushroom Soup

Roasted chestnuts make this mushroom soup silky. Roast them yourself or use store-bought chestnuts, which come cooked and peeled in vacuum-sealed bags. Choose seasonal wild mushrooms, or combine wild ones with cultivated button, oyster and shiitake mushrooms.

(Serves 6)

2 tbsp olive oil

1 cup (250 ml) chopped leeks

1 cup (250 ml) chopped celery

2 cups (500 ml) sliced mushrooms

salt and freshly ground pepper

4 cups (1 l) chicken stock

1 cup (250 ml) chestnuts, roasted and peeled

3 tbsp chopped fresh parsley

1 tbsp butter

For garnish:

35 per cent cream

pine nuts, toasted

Heat olive oil in a large saucepan over medium heat and add leeks and celery. Sauté, stirring, until leeks are translucent and celery is softened. Add half the mushrooms and cook until tender, about 10 minutes. Season with salt and pepper. Add chicken stock and roasted chestnuts and bring to a boil. Reduce heat and simmer for 20 minutes. Leave soup to cool slightly, then purée in small batches in a blender.

Meanwhile, sauté remaining mushrooms and parsley in butter over medium-high heat until mushrooms are slightly crisp and lightly browned.

Ladle warm soup into bowls and garnish with swirls of cream, sautéed mushroom and pine nuts.

Roasting chestnuts

- - -

Around the world, sweet, starchy chestnuts are boiled or roasted for savoury dishes and desserts. It is their smooth, fudgy texture that is so irresistible.

To roast chestnuts, cut them open slightly to allow steam to escape as they cook: with a sharp paring knife, make a slit or an X on the flat side of each nut. Place the chestnuts in a single layer in a long-handled, perforated chestnut roaster or an aluminum pie plate with holes punched in it. Place your pan on a grill over the fire. Turn the chestnuts every few minutes, cooking until the shells begin to curl away from the flesh around the X. This should take about 15 minutes. Chestnuts can also be roasted, uncovered, in a preheated 350°F (180°C) oven for about 20 minutes. They are ready when the shells begin to curl.

When chestnuts are cool enough to handle, peel off the shells and inner skins. (Peeling only gets harder when the chestnuts cool completely.) Eat them warm with a glass of wine or set aside for another use.

· CRANBERRYVILLE ·

St-Louis-de-Blandford

Most of the year, St-Louis-de-Blandford is a plain little town straddling Highway 20 on the way to Quebec City. Come October, though, it sheds its dull cloak for a breathtaking show. As far as the eye can see, the landscape is transformed into a shimmering sea of jewel-tone red against a backdrop of golden birch and larch. It's like stepping into a Mark Rothko painting.

Sandy fields of knee-high cranberry bushes are flooded with water from the nearby Bécancourt River. Mammoth mechanical harvesters move in, straddling the rows, shaking the submerged foliage, sending the bright-red berries dancing into the air and splashing back down to weave a floating red carpet. Farm workers in hip waders, ear muffs and insulated rubber gloves wade through the cranberry bogs' frigid water, raking the berries, then pumping them into waiting trucks. When the 40-day harvest is done at the end of October, they will have gathered more than 23 million pounds of fruit in and around St-Louis-de-Blandford.

Cranberries are hardy nordic plants; long ago Quebec's indigenous tribes picked them from the forests near here. Atoka, they called them. But now at the 900-acre Ferme Bieler and 60 or so smaller farms nearby, the wild cranberry has been upstaged by a hardy cultivated cousin called Stephens.

St-Louis-de-Blandford's fresh cranberries light up the fading landscape at Jean Talon Market in late fall. And the handwritten signs declaring their provenance put a little town on the map in the big city. But these bushels and baskets are but a fraction of the harvest. Ninety per cent of the cranberries will be frozen or pressed into juice, destined for the United States, Europe, Saudi Arabia and China, where the sour berry's antioxidant properties have made it a star.

Ferme Bieler, St-Louis-de-Blandford

November's Tart

Tangy cranberries shimmer atop this tart with a nutty crust and creamy filling. Use fresh cranberries when they come to market in late fall or frozen ones at any other time.

(Serves 8 to 10)

For cranberry topping:
3 cups (750 ml) cranberries, fresh or frozen
¾ cup (180 ml) maple syrup
finely grated zest and juice of 2 oranges
1 cinnamon stick (optional)

For crust:
1¼ cups (310 ml) flour
¾ cup (180 ml) sugar
½ cup (125 ml) butter, softened
½ cup (125 ml) ground pecans

For filling:
2 8-oz (250 g) packages cream cheese, softened
¼ cup (60 ml) orange juice
½ cup (125 ml) sugar

Preheat oven to 350°F (180°C).
To make topping, combine cranberries, maple syrup, orange zest and juice and cinnamon in a medium saucepan. Cook over medium heat, stirring gently to avoid breaking up the cranberries as they pop. Cook about 5 minutes, until cranberries are soft and glaze has thickened. Remove from heat and cool completely.

Meanwhile, make crust. In a large, shallow bowl mix together flour and sugar. Cut in butter using a fork or pastry blender until mixture resembles coarse crumbs. Stir in nuts. Press mixture into an ungreased 10-inch (25 cm) round tart pan with a removable fluted rim, making sure to press dough evenly all the way up the sides. Bake in middle of oven for 15 minutes, or until light gold around the edges. Remove from oven and transfer to a rack to cool.

While tart shell bakes, make filling. In a large bowl, using an electric mixer at medium speed, cream the softened cream cheese with orange juice and sugar until smooth. Spread filling into cooled tart shell and bake for another 15 minutes, until filling has set. Remove to rack to cool.

Spread cranberry topping over tart. Just before serving, carefully remove rim of tart pan.

Apple Ginger Pork Shoulder

Pork shoulder is a flavourful and inexpensive cut of meat that practically guarantees a tender and succulent roast as long as it is cooked long and slow. Its ample layer of fat and collagen keeps the meat moist.

(Serves 4 to 6)
For rub:

3 cloves garlic, crushed

zest of 1 lemon

1 tbsp finely grated fresh ginger

1 tbsp finely chopped fresh rosemary

2 tsp salt

1 tsp freshly ground black pepper

1 tbsp extra-virgin olive oil

For roast:

3- to 4-lb (1.5 kg) boneless pork shoulder

1 large onion, thickly sliced

4 apples, sliced but not peeled

1 cup (250 ml) apple cider

Glazed Carrots

Carrots are sublime roasted in the oven with a little sweetness and spice.

(Serves 6)

2 tbsp olive oil

1 tsp ground cumin

½ tsp cinnamon

½ tsp salt

freshly ground pepper

2 lb (1 kg) carrots, peeled and cut

3 tbsp pomegranate syrup (or honey)

½ cup (125 ml) dried cranberries

1 tbsp lemon juice

¼ cup (60 ml) chopped fresh parsley

Preheat oven to 325°F (160°C).
To make rub, combine garlic, lemon zest, ginger, rosemary, salt, pepper and olive oil.

Place meat skin-side up on a board and pat dry with a paper towel. With a knife, score the skin in a crosshatch pattern, making sure not to cut through to the meat. With your fingers, rub pork shoulder with the prepared rub, massaging it into the meat and pushing it into the folds. Place the pork skin-side up in a roasting pan and surround with onion and apple slices. Pour apple cider into the bottom of the pan.

Roast, uncovered, for 3½ hours or until the meat is completely tender. Spoon juices over the top of the roast at regular intervals. When pork is done, an instant-read thermometer inserted into the centre of the roast should register 150°F (65°C). Let the roast sit before pulling it apart with a fork and knife into shredded pieces. Serve with the slices of apple and onion and spoonfuls of pan juices.

Preheat oven to 400°F (200°C).
In a large, shallow ovenproof baking pan, combine olive oil, cumin, cinnamon, salt and pepper. Add carrots and pomegranate syrup and toss until coated. Roast in oven 45 minutes, turning occasionally, until carrots are fork-tender and caramelized. Toss with cranberries and sprinkle with lemon juice and parsley.

· THE UNLIKELY ENTREPRENEURS ·

James Henry Atkins & Charles Atkins

They were long-haired hippies, those Atkins brothers, when they arrived in this isolated fishing hamlet in the Gaspé. Who knew they would stay to become one of the village's largest employers?

James Henry was a laid-back philosophy graduate just back from the West Coast, where he had spent five years fishing, logging and tree planting. He was visiting a cousin here when he found himself in L'Anse-Pleureuse, on Gaspé's north shore. "Weeping cove" is how the name translates, and James Henry fell hard for the wooden cottages painted red, pink and turquoise that cling to the shoreline like beads on a necklace. There was a century-old house on the hill for sale at an incredibly low price, on land that rises into the Chic-Choc Mountains on one side and overlooks the St. Lawrence River on the other. James Henry called his brother Charles, who had been wandering around Mexico, and suggested they pool their money to buy it.

And so they did, thinking they would make a living logging and fishing. But that was easier said than done, and their unemployment cheques were running out. They needed a plan. During this time, they had begun smoking a little salmon. They used an old fridge in the chicken coop, rigging it up as a smoker; a camping stove and a cast-iron pan filled with moistened sawdust created just the right amount of smoke. James Henry got a grant from a local business development office. Then he persuaded the grocer in nearby Mont-Louis to move aside his poultry to make room for the Atkins brothers' smoked fish. They bought Atlantic salmon from New Brunswick and mackerel and shrimp from the local fisherman who unloaded right there in Mont-Louis. The brothers would smoke the fish once a month, then use the revenues to buy the next batch of fish. And so on. The business grew. People who tasted their smoked salmon fillet spread the word. Soon they built their own smokehouse with a small store attached to it. Now they do more than $2 million worth of business a year, at their store in Jean Talon Market and through distributors in Quebec and New York City.

James Henry recalls all this on the porch of the house in L'Anse-Pleureuse, where he has lived now for more than 20 years. He and brother Charles, who lives down the road, are lingering over a late lunch of smoked scallops and squid accompanied by glasses of porter and chasers of scotch. "I was a hippie and a bon vivant when I got here," James Henry says. "I'm still a bon vivant. But who ever thought I'd become a businessman?"

Charles & James-Henry
Vitous-Clémence Samson

Smoked Fish Chowder

When a chill sets in, a thick bowl of seafood chowder studded with mussels, shrimp, potato and smoked mackerel hits the spot.

(Serves 4 to 6)

8 oz (225 g) bacon, chopped

2 medium onions, chopped

3 stalks celery, chopped

2 bay leaves

2 tbsp flour

½ cup (125 ml) white wine

2 cups (500 ml) fish stock or bottled clam juice

3 medium potatoes, peeled and cut into ½-inch (1 cm) cubes

1 lb (500 g) mussels, scrubbed and debearded

1 lb (500 g) small to medium-size shrimp, shelled

8 oz (225 g) smoked mackerel fillets, broken into bite-size pieces

1 cup (250 ml) whole milk

freshly ground black pepper

½ cup (125 ml) finely chopped fresh parsley

Heat a heavy-bottomed casserole over medium-high heat and add bacon. Cook until crisp and remove with a slotted spoon. Drain all but 1 tbsp of bacon fat from pan and add onion, celery and bay leaves. Cook until vegetables are softened but not browned. Reduce heat to medium, sprinkle vegetables with flour and whisk until combined. Sauté for 2 minutes or until golden. Add wine and cook, stirring constantly, for about 5 minutes or until reduced by half. Add fish stock or clam juice and potatoes; cook for 15 minutes or until potatoes are tender. Add mussels, shrimp and smoked fish, reduce heat and simmer for another 5 minutes, until mussels have opened (discard any that have not) and shrimp is pink and cooked through. Remove bay leaves and discard.

Stir in milk and heat gently without boiling. Season with pepper. Ladle into bowls and scatter with parsley.

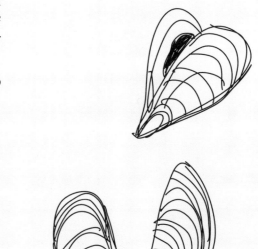

Lonzo
morceaux: 4,50$/100g
tranché: 6$/100g

le BlackBurn
47,50 kg

LOUIS
D'OR
50,60 $/kg

LAIT
CRU
Bio

– WINTER –

(Rest)

....

The holidays are coming and the market feels festive. The vendors have ordered giant wheels of cheese, and turkey, goose and pork for roasting. Cookie bakers and fruitcake makers dart in and out for hunks of chocolate and candied cherries. Their bags bulge with flour and sugar. The fruit sellers' tables are piled with burnished mahogany chestnuts from southern Italy, pomegranates from Spain, and hillocks of fresh local cranberries.

Outside, where the tomato sellers used to be, a forest of fresh-cut balsam firs perfumes the air. These *sapins* are Québécois favourites. The treesellers in toques and fur-lined mittens have a Christmas tree for every taste, from knee-high cash-and-carry saplings to five-metre mammoths fit for a mansion.

Only half the market's outdoor vendors come inside for winter – into the long, narrow covered hall that is Jean Talon Market's cold-weather shelter. The rest go home to rest and recuperate, or move on to other work to pay the bills until spring. Those who stick around supplement their offerings with imports. A principled few restrict themselves to the refrigerated apples, beets and brassicas they themselves grew.

Though the winter market lacks the exuberance of its summer self, there is a cocoon-like coziness to Jean Talon Market in Siberian mid-February, when the day is dark and windows are frosted. Or early on a blizzardy Saturday morning, when the rest of the city is stuck in snowbanks or snuggled in bed. Inside, the market feels like a world unto itself, cast in the ethereal glow of fluorescent lights and the mingling aromas of coffee roasting and sausages smoking. A frothy bowl of café au lait at the *brûlerie* warms cold hands before a foray in search of beef and onions for braising, apples for pie-baking.

What's amazing is the variety of local fare in the depths of winter, in a northern land buried under ice and snow from December to April. The market's aisles are stacked with bushels of apples, orange mesh bags of onions, turnips, carrots and enough potatoes to last until next summer. There is smoked fish, charcuterie, fresh-baked *fougasse* and flaky *chocolatines*, gold-medal cheese, ice cider and *crème de cassis*. And it is Québécois, *de chez nous*.

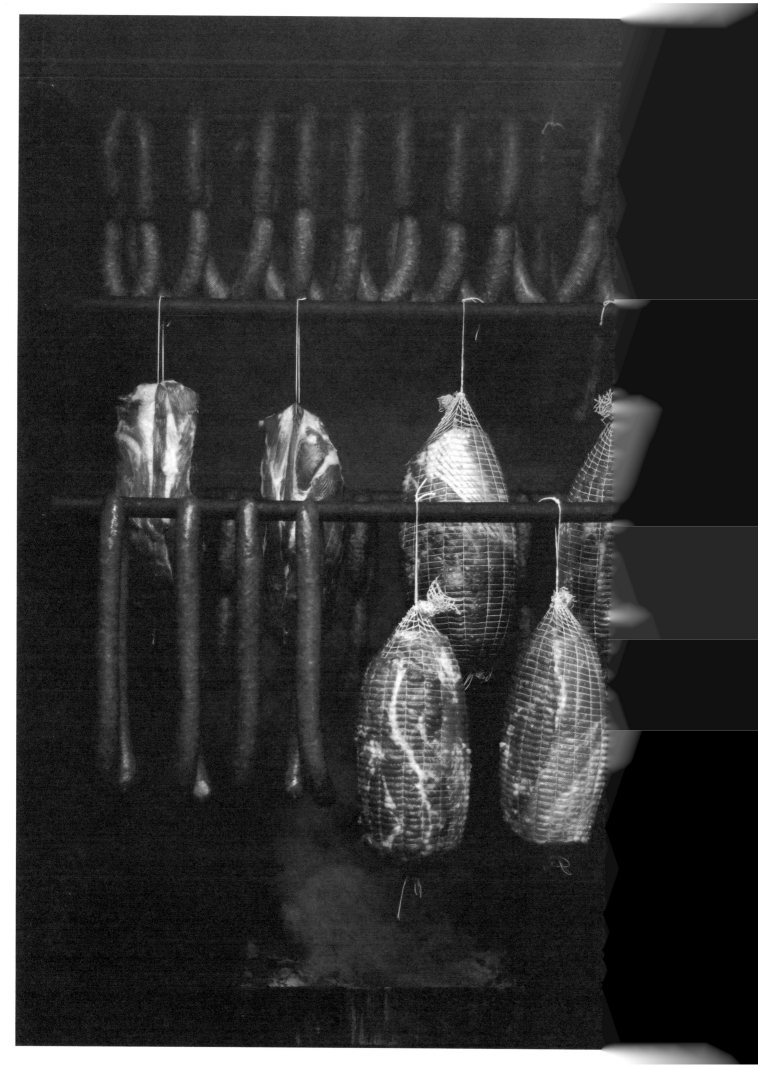

Back to our roots (& tubers)

Since ancient times, parsnips, turnips and Jerusalem artichokes have been winter staples, stored in root cellars or buried in pits under mounds of insulating snow. But during the war years, root vegetables earned a reputation as poor man's food. Gradually, they were sidelined by green vegetables arriving year-long from warmer climates. Soon they were thoroughly outdone by exotic alternatives like eggplants and yellow peppers.

Now, old-fashioned roots are back in vogue. Steamed and puréed for soup or roasted until caramel-gold, root vegetables are hearty and nutritious winter fare. Jacques Rémillard's motley collection of heirloom roots and tubers may be a mystery to many younger customers. But they make old-timers smile with nostalgia.

Jerusalem artichokes have nothing to do with the Holy Land; nor are they artichokes. They are the tubers from a native species of North American sunflower, called sunchokes in the United States and *topinambours* in French. Red-tinged knobs resembling gingerroot, they are nutty and sweet, almost garlicky. They can be thinly sliced, raw, into salads; or boiled in broth and puréed with orange zest for a velvety soup. An even simpler idea: wash well, then roast them whole. Sprinkle with sea salt and eat like potatoes in their skins.

Rutabagas and turnips are close cousins, often confused. Turnip is the little guy, smooth and white-fleshed with purple-tinged skin. Young turnips are sweet, but the taste sharpens as the vegetable ages. Rutabaga is larger, with a rough skin. Its flesh is yellow and sweeter than turnip. Both are delicious boiled and mashed with butter.

Bulbous and hairy, **celeriac** – or celery root – looks like the back of an old man's head. But peeled and grated, with mayonnaise and a little Dijon mustard, it is transformed into the classic French salad *céleri rémoulade*.

Parsnip resembles a stubby, cream-coloured carrot with a pungent smell. It needs the first frost of fall to develop its sweetness. The ancient Romans believed parsnips to be an aphrodisiac. Ukrainian grandmothers chop them up and add them to chicken soup, along with a handful of dill. You can also cut them into spears and roast with a splash of olive oil and a grating of ginger.

Parsley root looks like parsnip, only longer and more tapered. Its flesh is white, with a clean, fresh smell. It is usually sold in bunches with the leaves still on. Great cooked and mashed with potatoes.

Salsify is a long, thin baton with black skin covering white flesh. Its flavour is its most distinctive characteristic: like a cross between oysters and artichokes. Steam and serve with a vinaigrette or sauté in butter.

Beet Risotto

Ruby-red beets lend this risotto drama. It is a spectacular way to use an underappreciated vegetable. Crumbling goat cheese on top adds a tangy counterpoint. The key to creamy risotto is to add the liquid gradually and to stir continuously, making sure the rice doesn't stick to the bottom of the pot.

(Serves 4)

5 cups (1.25 l) good-quality chicken or vegetable broth

2 tbsp extra-virgin olive oil

2 tbsp butter

1 large onion, finely chopped

2 cloves garlic, crushed

3 medium beets, peeled and coarsely grated (about 2 cups/500 ml)

2 cups (500 ml) chopped spinach leaves

1½ cups (375 ml) short-grain Italian rice (like arborio or carnaroli)

salt and freshly ground pepper

½ cup (125 ml) dry white wine

1 tbsp finely chopped fresh rosemary

1 tbsp fresh thyme leaves

½ cup (125 ml) finely grated Parmesan cheese

4 oz (115 g) soft unripened goat cheese

fresh rosemary and thyme sprigs for garnish

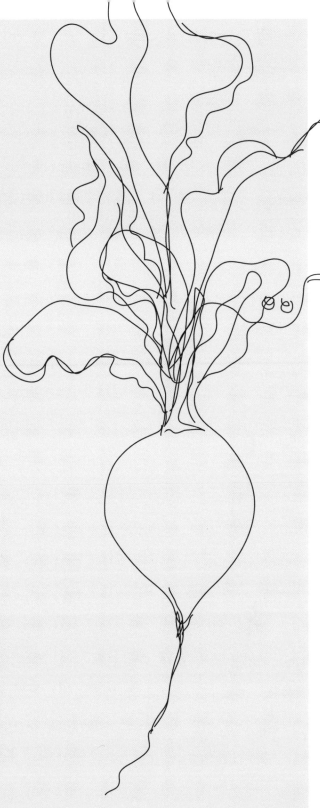

In a saucepan, heat the broth and keep it warm.

In a large, heavy-bottomed pot, melt olive oil with 1 tbsp of the butter and sauté onion, garlic and beets over medium-low heat until tender, about 8 minutes. Add spinach and cook until wilted, another 2 minutes or so.

Add rice and stir to coat the grains, sautéing gently for a minute or so. Add salt and a liberal grinding of pepper. Pour in wine and continue to cook, stirring, until it has evaporated. Add a ladleful of warm broth and stir constantly until all the liquid has been absorbed. Repeat – adding the broth a ladleful at a time, stirring constantly, always at a simmer over low heat – until all the broth is used up. This should take about 20 minutes. The rice should be al dente – moist and tender but still firm. Add extra broth if necessary.

Turn off the heat and stir in chopped rosemary, thyme, Parmesan cheese and the remaining 1 tbsp of butter. Taste and adjust seasoning. Serve immediately in shallow bowls with crumbled goat cheese and herb sprigs on top.

· THE TRAVELLERS ·

Ethné & Philippe de Vienne

In a few days Ethné and Philippe de Vienne will be zigzagging between Jaipur and Kerala, India, in a rented Jeep, on a mission to find white peppercorns and saffron. They are hunters who scour far-flung villages and night markets around the world in search of spices and sauces.

Their biggest deals go down in the oddest of places. Visiting a tribal king in a remote hamlet in Indonesia, the de Viennes followed local protocol and brought him a live chicken. That gift earned them an invitation to the village festival – and a slew of new Indonesian recipes. In Kashgar, in Central Asia, they stumbled on an ancient blend of Chinese, Indian and Persian spices when Ethné befriended a hotel receptionist who invited them back to his family's mud house. In a kitchen redolent with the smells of fennel, ginger, rosebud and star anise, Philippe stirred pots and scribbled notes while the women of the house shared their recipe for a lamb and fruit pilaf and Uyghur-style noodles. Their discoveries that day went on to become one of their best-selling spice mixes.

Their two shops at the market, La Dépense and Olives et Épices, are a jumble of barrels and woven baskets, the aromas of Provençal lavender and Indian cumin mingling in the air. Manu Chao sings in Portuguese and Spanish on the stereo and Buddhist prayer flags flutter from the ceiling.

 They travel light on their many trips. Ethné leaves her bag half-empty – space for bringing home silks and jewels and, of course, samples of the spice shipments that will arrive in Montreal by boat weeks later. Philippe's list of essentials is brief: duct tape for bandaging a sprained ankle or repairing a leaky canoe; pocket knives to offer as tokens of friendship; a first aid kit; a bottle of scotch for sealing a deal or taking the edge off a bad day.

He is an ex-caterer with a wide girth and a golden touch in the kitchen. She is a tall, willowy Trinidadian, a former model who makes her entrance in gemstones and embroidered jackets from the souks and silk shops of Istanbul and Bangkok. She laughs at his worst jokes; he lets her boss him around. They finish each other's sentences.

"We chat, we explore, we wander around," Ethné explains. "We never know where we'll end up or what we'll find there."

Ethne & Philippe

Honey Cake

This tawny, moist honey cake can be baked as a cake or in individual paper liners in a muffin tin. Make sure the honey is liquid. If it isn't, warm it up, then cool slightly before using.

(Serves 6 to 8)

3 eggs, beaten

½ cup (125 ml) sugar

1 cup (250 ml) honey

½ cup (125 ml) vegetable oil

1 tsp baking powder

1 tsp baking soda

1½ cups (375 ml) flour

½ cup (125 ml) strong tea, cooled

Preheat oven to 300°F (150°C).

Line an 8-inch-square (2 l) baking pan with parchment paper and grease lightly with vegetable oil. Or line a muffin tin with 8 paper liners.

In a large bowl with an electric mixer, beat eggs with sugar at medium speed until pale and fluffy. Add honey and oil and mix until combined. In another bowl, sift together baking powder, baking soda and flour. Add to the batter half a cup at a time, alternating with the tea, mixing after each addition.

Spread batter evenly in prepared cake pan or muffin tin. Bake 60 minutes (40 minutes for individual cakelets), or until dark gold and a wooden skewer inserted in the centre comes out clean. Cool in pan and serve warm or at room temperature. (Wrapped well in plastic wrap or kept in an airtight container, the cake stays soft and moist for several days.)

Indian Masala Chai

A pot of sweet, milky Indian spiced tea, *masala chai*, fills the kitchen with the smells of cinnamon, cardamom and cloves. Like the chai sellers do in Mumbai or New Delhi, we pour the hot tea into glasses from up high so it froths a little. Spongy honey cake, infused with the colour and flavour of tea, is just the right accompaniment.

(Serves 2 to 4)

2 tbsp loose black tea, like Assam or Darjeeling

2 cups (500 ml) water

1 tbsp sugar

2 whole cloves

4 green cardamom pods, lightly crushed

1 2-inch (5 cm) cinnamon stick

1 cup (250 ml) whole milk

In a medium saucepan, combine all ingredients except milk. Bring to a boil, then lower heat and simmer 2 or 3 minutes. Add milk, simmer another minute, then remove from heat. Strain and pour into glasses or small cups. Add extra sugar, if desired.

Spice Blends: Like brushstrokes in a painting, spice blends give vibrancy to dishes. Of course, many of them are available ready-made, but there is a sensual pleasure in blending your own, playing with the colours and flavours. Grind whole spices using a mortar and pestle or an electric coffee grinder. Let the spice blends cool thoroughly, then store in airtight containers in a cool, dry place for up to three months.

Dukka

From Egypt comes this coarse blend of nuts, seeds and spices. Dip slices of fresh crusty bread into olive oil then *dukka* for an aromatic appetizer.

¼ cup (60 ml) hazelnuts

¼ cup (60 ml) sesame seeds

2 tbsp coriander seeds

2 tbsp cumin seeds

1 tsp fennel seeds

1 tsp dried thyme

½ tsp black peppercorns

1 tsp coarse sea salt

In a dry frying pan, toast hazelnuts and set aside. Then toast remaining ingredients, shaking the pan constantly to keep them from burning. Remove from heat and cool completely. Combine ingredients and grind to a coarse texture, in batches if necessary.

Montreal Steak Spice

Delicatessens, rotisseries and steak restaurants up and down the Main have made this spice blend famous. Of course, the old guys never give up their recipes; this is my approximation. Use it to season roast chicken or steaks destined for the barbecue. Strange to say, it is also extraordinary on quick-seared tuna and sautéed shrimp.

2 tsp coarse salt

1 tbsp ground black pepper

1 tbsp hot red pepper flakes

1 tbsp garlic powder

1 tbsp dried onion flakes

2 tsp mustard seeds, coarsely ground

Mix to combine.

Gomasio

Use white sesame seeds or black for this traditional Korean and Japanese seasoning, or a combination of the two. Nice in soups or salads, or sprinkled on fish, rice or noodles.

½ cup (125 ml) toasted sesame seeds

1 tsp sea salt

½ tsp hot red pepper flakes

Toss toasted sesame seeds with sea salt and hot pepper flakes. Grind very briefly.

Iranian Saffron and Rose Blend

This delicate Persian spice mix is lovely in rice pilafs or to season chicken or fish.

1 tsp saffron

½ tsp ground cinnamon

½ tsp ground cumin

½ tsp ground cardamom

1 tsp dried rose petals

¼ tsp freshly ground black pepper

½ teaspoon fine sea salt

Combine all ingredients.

· THE GODMOTHER ·

Anne Fortin

They come in from the market stalls with a tray of raspberries or a memory of their grandmother's apple pie. Is raspberry jam hard to make, they want to know? How do you bake *tarte Tatin*? To these nervous young cooks taking their first tentative steps in the kitchen, Anne Fortin is both culinary coach and godmother.

She is a lifelong gourmande and a passionate cook. Her bookstore, Librairie Gourmande, is devoted to the art, craft and love of cooking. It is a foodie's oasis, a sunny and inviting place lined floor to ceiling with cookbooks and gastronomic encyclopedias, chefs' memoirs and food magazines from around the world. Even the walls here are covered with food – still lifes and abstract drawings by up-and-coming Montreal artists of fruit, fish and table settings.

This is where cookbook authors come to sign their just-published works, where the cognoscenti go to order Ferran Adrià's 600-page tome about his famous restaurant in Spain, but also where beginners find the basics.

Fortin, who is herself a published cookbook author, says her newest customers are young, inexperienced cooks, a new generation rebelling against fast food and industrial ingredients. "Maybe they aren't cooking three times a day like their grandmothers did, but they are rediscovering their taste buds and their place in the kitchen," says Fortin, sipping tea during a mid-afternoon break. "And they want to have fun."

Slowly, Fortin helps them build their culinary repertoires. In early summer, when the market brims with strawberries, she shares easy recipes for jams and shortcakes. When winter sets in, she brings forth the newest baking books featuring ginger and chocolate.

Before long, Fortin's protégés will have graduated from apple crisp and meatloaf to crème brûlée and osso bucco.

Anne, Librairie Gourmande

· THE MEMORY KEEPERS ·

Daniel Joseph & Pavel Grigore

Daniel Joseph was 12 years old when he and his family left Romania, fleeing revolution. They settled in France, and Daniel did what immigrant teenagers do: he blended in, learning French and listening to American pop music. Then he made his way to Montreal to study business and "see the world." Working as a part-time restaurant delivery boy, Joseph met Pavel Grigore, a former butcher and fellow Romanian castaway who made old-fashioned sausages in a rigged-up smoker on his balcony; the smoky, spicy meat was a balm for the wistfulness that swept over him every now and then. On weekends, Grigore's place in Côte des Neiges would be packed with fellow Romanians lured by his *cabanos* sausage and paprika-fuelled beef and lamb *mici* patties.

Pretty soon, the business student and the butcher were in business. Balkani, their delicatessen at the market, is an emporium of all things eastern European, a shrine to the Old World foods of Romania and its Balkan and Slavic neighbours. The shelves are stocked with peppered salmon from Poland, Ukrainian borscht and sauerkraut from Hungary. There is plum and rose petal jam, sour-cherry syrup, and camomile and nettle teas from Romania – every jar and packet a portal to their past. "If I taste a spoonful of acacia honey I'm back in Calarasi where I grew up, inhaling the perfume from the blossoms in spring," Joseph says wistfully. "In my memory, it's all so peaceful and bucolic."

But when he goes back to Romania on holiday, it's all gone. "Everybody is watching satellite television and talking on cellphones. Eating hamburgers and Nutella, making money." Here he is, though, halfway across the world behind the counter in his grocery store, importing Romanian jam and safeguarding what used to be.

Joseph and Grigore make all their cold cuts themselves, according to Grigore's inherited recipes. No phosphates, no additives, no fillers. The meat soaks in spice-studded brine and then hangs to smoke over a smouldering fire fed with maple and oak kindling. On Thursdays at Balkani, when the smoker is filled with strings of sausage and ribs of pork, the medieval smell of spiced, smoking meat is potent enough to pull Romanian expatriates right off the street. All weekend long, the place is packed with shoppers speaking Romanian, arguing politics and soccer, picking up a pound or two of sausage. Getting a taste of home.

Daniel & Karel, Balkani Charcuterie

Braised Red Cabbage & Sausage

Sauerkraut and sausage is a classic eastern European combination. Here, red cabbage is braised with brown sugar and apple-cider vinegar. The mildly tart and slightly sweet flavour is a pleasing counterpoint to spicy sausage.

(Serves 4)

1 tbsp olive oil

1 onion, finely sliced

1 head red cabbage, cored and very thinly sliced

1/3 cup (80 ml) apple-cider vinegar

¼ cup (60 ml) water

1 tbsp brown sugar

1 bay leaf

2 tsp juniper berries, lightly crushed (optional)

salt and freshly ground pepper

8 spicy smoked pork sausages

hot mustard (optional)

Heat the oil in a large, heavy skillet over medium-high heat. Add onion and cabbage and cook, stirring occasionally, for 5 minutes. Add vinegar, water, brown sugar, bay leaf and juniper berries and stir. Bring to a boil, then lower heat and cover. Cook over low heat for 30 minutes, stirring occasionally, until cabbage is tender. Season with salt and pepper and set aside.

Preheat oven to 350°F (180°C).
Grill sausages on a ridged grill pan over high heat for 2 minutes, then flip and grill other side. Transfer to oven and bake 15 minutes or until cooked through. Serve with braised cabbage and a little hot mustard, if desired.

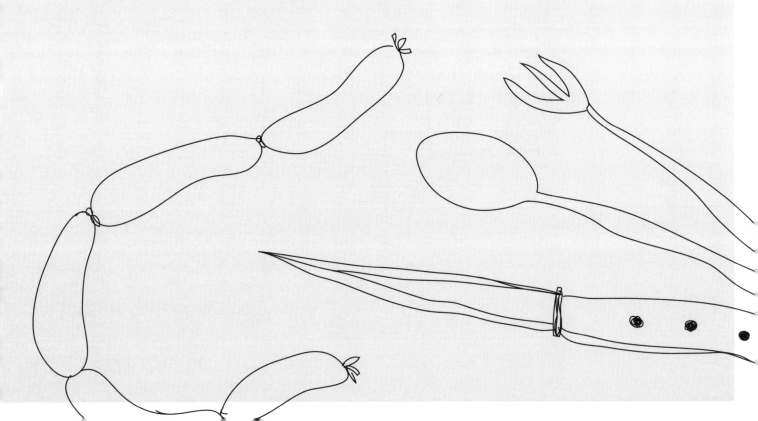

Tartiflette

This is a hearty potato dish for the depths of winter, when root vegetables are all that is left of last autumn's harvest. In Savoie, France, where *tartiflette* originated, it is served with cornichons and cured meats. Choose a soft raw-milk cheese with a washed rind, like Quebec's own Cru de Champlain, and a smoky, farm-cured bacon from the butcher.

(Serves 6)

6 large firm-fleshed potatoes, like Charlotte or Yukon Gold

salt and freshly ground pepper

1 lb (500 g) bacon, sliced into matchsticks

2 shallots, sliced

2 leeks, white parts only, sliced

3 tbsp chopped fresh thyme leaves

½ cup (125 ml) 35 per cent cream

1 lb (500 g) soft washed-rind cheese (like Reblochon or Cru de Champlain)

Wash and peel potatoes and boil for 15 minutes or until fork-tender. Drain, cool and cut into 1-inch (2 cm) slices. Season with salt and pepper.

Preheat oven to 375°F (190°C).
Sauté bacon, shallots, leeks and thyme in a frying pan until shallots and leeks are softened and bacon is crisp. Drain on paper towel.

Butter a gratin pan (or other shallow oven-proof dish) and line the bottom with a layer of sliced potatoes. Spread half the onion-bacon-thyme mixture on top. Add another layer of potatoes, followed by the rest of the onion and bacon. Pour on the cream. Cut the cheese in half crosswise and lay the two halves on top, rind-side up. Bake for 30 minutes, or until bubbling and golden on top. Remove from oven and let stand for 10 minutes before serving.

· THE BEEF FARMERS ·

Céline Bélec & Roger Raymond

Roger Raymond pulls himself out of bed in the velvety dark before dawn, pours a coffee and lumbers out the back door in his jacket and balaclava, big boots leaving a trail in the snow.

The herd will be hard to find in the blowing snow, but Raymond knows each of his animals by face and temperament and he has brought salt pellets as a treat to entice them. His 140 Angus cows are hulking, hardy animals that spend their days out of doors in all seasons, as cows used to in the days before industrial farming. They are pasture-raised and grass-fed, without growth hormones or antibiotics. That is a rarity in North America these days, where almost 90 per cent of cattle live their entire lives in barns, never once feeding on green grass under an open sky.

In extreme weather like this, Raymond's cows will be huddled under the spruce trees at the far reaches of Ferme Nordest, his 1,200-acre farm here in Mont-Laurier, a three-hour drive northwest of Montreal. Raymond bounces over the frozen fields in his all-terrain vehicle to herd the animals into a wooden shelter where his son David has piled mounds of homegrown hay, oats and barley for them to eat, as he does throughout winter. Otherwise, they roam free, grazing on wild grasses and fertilizing the fields, their manure encouraging future growth without the need for chemical fertilizers. In summer, when the weather is warm and the grass is at its most luscious, the cows give birth here in the pasture, too, and tend to their calves.

When the cattle have matured, within 20 months or so, they will be brought into an open stable for several months before slaughter, their diet supplemented with grain to enhance the meat's flavour, texture and fat content. In the butcher shop attached to the farmhouse, son Mathieu dry-ages sides of beef for 28 days before cutting them into steaks, shanks and roasts. Céline Bélec says her customers often tell her that Ferme Nordest's beef tastes "beefier" than the meat they buy at the supermarket. Her mother says it reminds her of the meat of her childhood. "I guess it's because we stick to the old-fashioned ways of our parents and grandparents," Bélec says.

Céline & Roger Mont-Laurier

Beer-Braised Beef

This slow-braised beef is inspired by Flemish carbonnade. Trois Pistoles, an almost-black Quebec microbrew, imparts chocolate and caramel notes to the dish. If you can, make it the day before and refrigerate, so the flavours have a chance to marry and excess fat can be removed. Reheat slowly and serve over potatoes or a root-vegetable mash.

(Serves 6)

3½-lb (1.5 kg) beef blade roast

salt and freshly ground pepper

3 tbsp olive oil

3 medium onions, chopped

2 carrots, chopped

5 cloves garlic, slivered

1 28-oz (796 ml) can tomatoes, including juice

2 12-oz (341 ml) bottles dark beer

1 cup (250 ml) beef broth

2 whole star anise

2 cinnamon sticks, 2 inches (5 cm) each

1 tsp whole peppercorns

4 bay leaves

8 sprigs fresh thyme

¼ cup (60 ml) Dijon mustard

3 tbsp finely chopped fresh parsley

Preheat oven to 325°F (160°C).
Season meat generously with salt and pepper. Heat oil in a large, heavy-bottomed ovenproof pot over medium-high heat. Add beef and cook, turning, until well browned, about 8 to 10 minutes per side. Remove meat to platter and set aside.

Add onion, carrots and garlic to pan and cook for a minute or 2, until onions are golden and carrots have begun to soften. Add tomatoes and their juice, beer, beef broth, star anise, cinnamon, peppercorns, bay leaves and thyme; stir. Bring to a boil, then return meat to pan. Cover and transfer to oven. Cook for 2½ to 3 hours or until beef is tender and falling off the bone.

Whisk in Dijon mustard and parsley and continue roasting, uncovered, until sauce has thickened, about 30 minutes. Remove from the oven and transfer to a platter, breaking meat into pieces. Taste the sauce and adjust seasoning. Pour over the meat.

Three-Root Mash

For creaminess, try a starchy potato, like russet, Chieftain or Yukon Gold. Use an old-fashioned potato masher for a chunky, rustic texture.

(Serves 6)

4 large potatoes, peeled and quartered

1 turnip, peeled and cut into chunks

4 medium carrots, peeled and cut up

3 tbsp butter

¾ cup (180 ml) whole milk

1 tbsp olive oil

3 shallots, chopped

1 clove garlic, crushed

salt and freshly ground pepper

In a pot of cold water, bring root vegetables to a boil. Simmer, uncovered, until tender, 15 to 20 minutes. Drain and return to pot. Add butter and milk and mash. Keep covered. Sauté shallots and garlic in olive oil until soft and pale gold, then add to mash. Season.

Pork and Orange Albondigas

Nickel-size meatballs are a tapas bar staple. These are easily made ahead and reheated in the oven. Serve on a platter with toothpicks.

(*Makes about 3 dozen*)

For meatballs:

¼ cup (60 ml) olive oil

1 small onion, finely chopped

2 tbsp pine nuts

2 cloves garlic, crushed

flour, for dusting

1 lb (500 g) ground pork

½ lb (250 g) ground veal

½ cup (125 ml) bread crumbs

finely grated zest of 1 orange

1 egg, lightly beaten

2 tbsp finely chopped fresh parsley

1 tsp ground fennel seeds

salt and freshly ground pepper

For sauce:

1 tbsp olive oil

1 small onion, finely chopped

1 garlic clove, crushed

1 cup (250 ml) canned tomatoes, chopped

¼ cup (60 ml) white wine

¼ cup (60 ml) orange juice

1 short cinnamon stick

To make meatballs: Heat 1 tbsp of the olive oil in a frying pan and cook the onion until soft. Add pine nuts and garlic and continue cooking until golden. Remove from heat to cool.

Spread flour on a plate and keep nearby. In a mixing bowl, combine onion mixture, pork, veal and other meatball ingredients. Form into bite-size balls, rolling each in the flour.

Heat remaining oil over medium-high heat and fry meatballs in batches, without crowding, turning several times, until browned all over. Remove to a paper-towel-lined tray to drain.

To make sauce: Sauté onion and garlic in olive oil until soft. Add tomatoes and their juice, wine, orange juice and cinnamon stick; simmer over medium heat until sauce thickens, about 10 minutes. Add meatballs to sauce and heat, stirring to coat.

To the market for tapas

\- - -

At the holidays, a casual get-together over wine or beer and an assortment of little plates is most convivial. Nothing fancy. The winter market is just the place to go foraging for the fixings. All you need, really, is smoked fish from Atkins et Frères and a few charcuterie meats – maybe *lonzo*, *figatelli* or a wine-cured *strolghino* from Les Cochons tout ronds. A packet of paper-thin prosciutto slices and an assortment of olives from Capitole; an armload of baguettes from the bakery. On to Fromagerie Hamel or Qui Lait Cru for a few hunks of good cheese to set out on a big wooden board. Time permitting, you could prepare a platter or two of homemade *amuse-gueules* to pass around.

Prosciutto & Ricotta Roulades

An easy Italian appetizer, enlivened with a few drops of balsamic vinegar.

(Makes 8)
1 cup (250 ml) ricotta cheese
2 tsp extra-virgin olive oil
¼ cup (60 ml) grated Parmesan cheese
salt and freshly ground pepper
1 tsp finely grated lemon zest
8 slices prosciutto
½ cup (125 ml) arugula leaves, washed and dried
balsamic vinegar, for drizzling

In a bowl, combine ricotta, olive oil, Parmesan cheese, salt, freshly ground pepper and lemon zest.

Lay prosciutto slices out flat on a clean work surface. Place a spoonful of ricotta mixture on each slice and top with a few arugula leaves. Drizzle with balsamic vinegar and roll up, securing with a toothpick.

Smoked Mackerel Rillette

Mackerel is an oily fish, excellent for smoking. It is divine puréed into a rillette, which can also be made with smoked trout. Serve it spread on toasted points of brown bread or on crackers.

(Enough for 12 canapés)
8 oz (225 g) smoked and peppered mackerel fillet, skinned
¼ cup (60 ml) crème fraîche or whipping cream
2 tbsp mayonnaise
1 tbsp prepared horseradish
juice of ½ lemon
2 tbsp finely chopped fresh chives
freshly ground pepper

Tear mackerel into pieces and pulse briefly in a food processor. Add remaining ingredients and purée until smooth.

Arctic Char Carpaccio

Arctic char from Ungava Bay is available fresh all year long. Its delicate pink flesh makes a silky carpaccio.

(Makes about 12 canapés)
1 lb (500 g) Arctic char fillet
¼ lb (125 g) cold-smoked salmon
¼ cup (60 ml) marinated hot peppers
2 tbsp capers, drained and chopped
2 tbsp finely chopped fresh dill
2 tbsp finely chopped fresh parsley
sea salt and freshly ground pepper
1 tbsp white wine vinegar
1 tbsp freshly squeezed lemon juice
2 tbsp extra-virgin olive oil

Slice Arctic char, smoked salmon and marinated hot peppers into thin strips. In a shallow bowl, combine all ingredients. Adjust seasonings if necessary. Serve immediately in small porcelain spoons or on croutons.

· THE ICEMAN ·

Pascal Lacroix

It's late January and the temperature hovers just above zero. It has been months since we smelled green grass or opened the windows, and most of us are basking in this rare break from winter's grip.

Not the Iceman. Pascal Lacroix seems happiest with frost biting at his ears. He skis, snowshoes, skates and ice fishes. The fur-lined flaps of his hat fly in the wind as he races his snowmobile. Ice is his element. It's his livelihood, too. Lacroix is an artisan of that most Québécois of inventions: ice cider, made from the juice of frozen apples harvested in the depths of winter.

This year's wild temperature fluctuations have wreaked havoc with his harvest. Without the usual hard frost in November to freeze the apples to their branches, many have fallen to the ground. And now this thaw, accompanied by gusting winds, has made matters worse. Bushels more apples in the hilltop orchard have dropped. Three-quarters of the harvest is lost. Lacroix trudges through knee-deep snow and plucks a wrinkled Cortland from a branch. It tastes of applesauce and brown sugar. But with these mild temperatures, it's too soft for cider-making. He and his brigade of parka-clad, snowshoed harvesters will have to wait another week or two, until the temperature dips to -12 or -15 Celsius and freezes the fruit hard.

Against a barren backdrop of white and brown and grey, russet-coloured apples clinging like Christmas ornaments to bare, gnarled branches are a magical sight. The Lacroix family has been tending apple trees here in St-Joseph-du-Lac, northwest of Montreal, for four generations. Pascal bought this hilly, 14-hectare parcel two decades ago and set about planting 5,000 apple trees. The fruits of their labour bring busloads of apple-picking schoolchildren and pick-your-own customers in the fall. But it is their ice cider that has won them international acclaim – and a neckful of medals from international competitions. In a good year, Lacroix's cider house produces a thousand litres of honey-gold and amber-hued ciders, with their complex notes of tarte Tatin and ginger, almond and mango, caramel and cinnamon. But in a bad winter like this one, Lacroix watches helplessly as the bulk of his harvest turns to mush beneath the trees. "That's the hardship with ice cider. But it's the beauty, too. It's what gives it romance and mystery."

Pascal, St-Joseph-du-Lac

Ice Cider Pork Tenderloin

This is a recipe from the Lacroix family, whose apple trees dot the winter landscape in St-Joseph-du-Lac. Serve with rice pilaf and sautéed spinach with apples.

(Serves 4)

2 pork tenderloins (1½ lb/750 g total)

salt and freshly ground pepper

2 tbsp olive oil

¼ cup (60 ml) ice cider

2 tbsp finely chopped fresh rosemary leaves

1 tbsp whole-grain mustard

½ cup (125 ml) 35 per cent cream

Cut tenderloin fillets crosswise into medallions about 1 inch (2 cm) thick. Pound them to flatten slightly. Season liberally with salt and pepper. Heat oil in a large, heavy frying pan and cook the medallions over medium heat, in a single layer without crowding, for 3 minutes on each side, until nicely browned. Remove to a platter and keep warm.

Still over medium heat, add ice cider and rosemary to pan and deglaze, bringing to a boil and scraping up the brown bits, until reduced by half. Add mustard and cream and cook over medium-high heat another 2 to 3 minutes, stirring often, until sauce thickens. Return medallions to pan and toss to coat with sauce. Serve immediately.

Parsley Rice Pilaf

The perfect pilaf is loose and fluffy. To get it right, three steps are essential: wash the rice; heat the broth; cover with a clean dishtowel to absorb excess moisture.

(Serves 4)

1½ cups (375 ml) basmati rice

2 cups (500 ml) chicken or vegetable broth

2 tbsp butter or olive oil

1 onion, finely chopped

1 cup (250 ml) chopped fresh parsley

salt and freshly ground pepper

Using a sieve, rinse rice under running water. Drain and repeat. In a bowl, cover the rice with cold water and soak for 15 to 20 minutes. Drain.

Heat broth. In a large pot with a tight-fitting lid, heat butter or olive oil over medium heat. Add onion and sauté a couple of minutes. Add rice, stir, and cook for a minute or so. Add warm broth and bring to a boil. Stir, then cover and reduce heat to very low. Cook without stirring 15 minutes or until liquid is absorbed. Remove from heat. Add parsley, cover pot with a clean, dishtowel and replace lid. Let stand 10 to 15 minutes. Fluff with a fork, mixing in parsley, and season with salt and pepper.

Apple & Pine Nut Spinach

(Serves 4)

2 tbsp olive oil

2 medium shallots, chopped

1 clove garlic, crushed

1 large apple, peeled and chopped

½ cup (125 ml) raisins

8 cups (2 l) baby spinach leaves

2 tbsp freshly squeezed lemon juice

¼ cup (60 ml) toasted pine nuts

Heat olive oil in a frypan over medium-high heat. Add shallots and garlic and sauté until tender. Add apple and cook until golden. Stir in raisins and spinach. Cover and cook just until wilted. Serve with lemon juice, scattered with pine nuts.

· THE AMBASSADORS ·

Mohamed Rekik & Saoussen Frikha

The smell alone will transport you. Step inside L'Olivier, under a canopy of woven baskets and past a clutter of copper pots, conical tajines and hand-painted platters, and you have entered a North African souk, with its bright colours and mingling aromas of lemon, orange blossom, hot pepper and olive brine.

Mohamed Rekik, a mechanical engineer who also happens to be a born salesman, presides over the cash. He issues orders to the phalanx of butchers at the back. He banters in a pastiche of Arabic and French with customers who squeeze through the serpentine aisles in search of olive oil, couscous, dried fruits and nuts. He and his wife Saoussen Frikha have re-created the atmosphere of the market stalls back in Sfax, Tunisia, their hometown. They stock silver teapots, gold-etched glasses and fresh mint for Moroccan tea. They sell flaky pastry for fried *briks* and sticky braided sweets called *chebakia*. Vats of preserved lemons, olives and fuchsia-pink pickled turnips are ready for ladling into take-away containers.

Frikha, a biologist and trained naturopath, stations herself by the spice shelf. She shares recipes, explains to the Montreal-born how olives are harvested, demystifies the ingredients in *tabil* and *ras el hanout* spice mixes.

At first the couple's only goal was to make a modest living providing a meeting place for the Algerians, Moroccans and Tunisians who come to Montreal from the Maghreb region of North Africa. But now, Rezik says, his woollen *chachia* cap perched on his head as usual, they also want to be Maghreb ambassadors, sharing Tunisian music, sipping Moroccan mint tea with those who have never tried it, extolling the virtues of halal meat.

Saoussen & Mohamed, L'Olivier

Lubia, a Moroccan Bean Stew

This is a hearty cold-weather dish of slow-simmered dried beans, infused with the flavours of North Africa. Start the night before by soaking the dried beans – either lima beans, white kidney beans or the smaller navy beans or light green French flageolets. Simmered long and gentle in a spicy broth, the beans lend the stew a thick, creamy consistency. It can be made with or without meat.

(Serves 8)

1 tbsp baking soda

2 cups (500 ml) dried beans

2 tbsp olive oil

2 lb (1 kg) beef short ribs (optional)

3 onions, chopped

6 cloves garlic, finely chopped

1 tbsp hot paprika

2 tsp ground cumin

½ tsp crumbled saffron

2 bay leaves

3 large tomatoes, coarsely chopped

salt and freshly ground pepper

Dissolve baking soda in a large bowl filled with 4 quarts (4 litres) cold water. Pick over and rinse the beans. Add them to the water, making sure they are completely covered. Leave to soak at room temperature for at least 8 hours or up to 24 hours. Drain and rinse well.

Heat the oil in a large, heavy-bottomed soup pot over medium-high heat. Add the meat, if using, and brown lightly on all sides. Add onion and cook, stirring, until softened. Add garlic, paprika, cumin, saffron and bay leaves and cook, stirring, for a few minutes more.

Add tomatoes and drained beans, salt to taste and a liberal grinding of pepper. Cover generously with water, bring to a boil, skim the surface, then reduce heat to low. Simmer gently for 2 hours, stirring occasionally, until the beans are tender and the sauce has thickened, adding water if necessary. Garnish with fresh parsley. Serve with thick slices of warm bread.

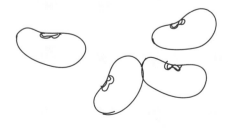

Orange Blossom Semolina Cake

Sweet almond and semolina cakes are popular throughout the Middle East and North Africa. They go by many names – *sfouf, basbousa, namoura*. This cake, soaked with zesty lemon syrup and studded with almonds, is pure sunshine on a grey winter's day. The flavours – orange flower water, lemon and tahini – are straight from the soukh. All the ingredients are available at the North African shops flanking the market's edges.

For the syrup:

1 cup (250 ml) sugar

1 cup (250 ml) water

¼ cup (60 ml) freshly squeezed lemon juice (from 1 lemon)

4 tbsp orange flower water

1 tbsp butter

For the cake:

4 tbsp tahini

1½ cups (375 ml) medium-ground semolina

¼ cup (60 ml) sugar

1 tsp ground cinnamon

1 tsp baking soda

½ tsp salt

1 cup (250 ml) plain yogurt

3 tbsp butter, melted

½ cup (125 ml) whole blanched almonds

Preheat oven to 375°F (190°C).

To prepare syrup: Mix sugar and water in a medium-size saucepan and bring to a boil, stirring to dissolve sugar. Lower heat and simmer until slightly thickened, about 10 minutes. Remove from heat. Stir in lemon juice, orange flower water and butter.

To prepare cake: Butter a 13-by-9-inch (3.5 l) rectangular cake pan with the tahini, making sure to cover bottom and sides. In a medium-size mixing bowl, beat together all the other ingredients except the almonds. (The dough will be thick.) Spread dough into prepared cake pan and let sit at room temperature for 30 minutes.

Top with almonds and bake 30 minutes, or until golden. Remove cake from oven and cut into squares, leaving them in the baking dish. While cake is still hot, pour the syrup over it.

Moroccan tea

- - -

Moroccans drink mint tea throughout the day: when friends drop by, during business negotiations, or anytime sweets are offered. Preparing and serving the tea is social tradition and every household owns a tea tray with an ornate silver teapot and painted glasses. Custom dictates that the host pour the sweet tea into small glasses, aerating the brew by pouring from on high. Guests must take at least three sips before leaving.

To make Moroccan mint tea: steep 2 tsp Chinese gunpowder green tea in 4 cups (1 l) of boiling water for 2 minutes. Add sugar to taste and a dozen or so fresh mint leaves. Let stand 3 or 4 minutes and serve.

To make a refreshing iced tea, add a splash of orange blossom water and serve on ice.

· THE SHEPHERDS ·

Lucille Giroux & Alastair MacKenzie

More than three decades and dozens of international awards later, it doesn't look quite so crazy. But when Lucille Giroux and her husband, Richard Caisse, first drove through the hills of Bois Franc and into the sleepy village of Ste-Hélène-de-Chester, with its cedar-shingle cottages and ramshackle barns, a kind of madness fell upon them. By the time the holiday was over, they had bought a farm and made a pact to quit their jobs and sell their suburban home to become shepherds. "It was a real *coup de foudre*. Love at first sight," Giroux recalls, as she works in the white-tiled aging cave, poking holes into rounds of ripening blue cheese, encouraging the blue-green bacteria that will give her Bleu de la Moutonnière its salty zest. "We knew we wanted to be in the country, but we had not a shred of farming knowledge," she admits.

Giroux imported a flock of East Friesian dairy sheep from Europe. She became the first sheep's-milk cheesemaker in the province, bringing her blue cheese and feta to another *fromagerie* to be aged and selling it at nearby shops and farmers' markets. But it was proving to be more work than she had anticipated. So when a New Zealand sheep farmer came into the picture and proposed a partnership, Giroux accepted.

Alastair MacKenzie had been tending sheep on his family's New Zealand farm since he was 8. A different kind of love-at-first-sight brought him here: He fell for a Québécoise who had come to New Zealand on vacation and beckoned him to follow her home. So here he is, rugged and relaxed, in the fading light of La Moutonnière's whitewashed barn, surrounded by 130 bleating white ewes and fleecy lambs who recognize his voice and amble over for a handful of barley.

In spring and summer, when the sheep are out grazing on red and white clover and dandelion in the hilly pastures, MacKenzie has only to whistle for them to come in for milking. In the fall, he leaves the barn doors open so they can come in on cold nights. By early December, they know not to venture out into the cold, and MacKenzie shuts the barn door behind them, opening it again come spring when the weather warms.

It didn't take long before Giroux and Mackenzie began winning awards. Now, every week a truckful of sheep's-milk cheeses and creamy yogurt, as well as socks and hats knitted from their sheeps' wool, heads into the city.

Lucille & Alastair Ste-Hélène-de-Chester

Crunchy Granola

This granola is dense with oats, nuts, seeds and dried fruit and is high in fibre, antioxidants and the omega-3 fatty acids found in flaxseeds. For breakfast, serve it it on yogurt with whatever fruit is in season. In winter, I like to pile on matchstick slivers of apple or pomegranate seeds – and then finish with a drizzle of maple syrup or honey. Greek- or Balkan-style sheep's milk yogurt is luxuriously thick. It also happens to be richer in protein, calcium and other minerals and vitamins than cow's milk yogurt.

(Makes 5 cups (1.25 l))

2 cups (500 ml) old-fashioned rolled oats

pinch of salt

1 tsp cinnamon

½ tsp nutmeg

1/3 cup (80 ml) maple syrup

3 tbsp canola or sunflower oil

½ cup (125 ml) shelled, coarsely chopped pistachios

¼ cup (60 ml) flaxseeds

½ cup (125 ml) pumpkin seeds

½ cup (125 ml) sunflower seeds

1 cup (250 ml) dried cranberries

1 cup (250 ml) chopped dried apricots

Preheat oven to 325°F (160°C).

Line a baking sheet with parchment paper. In a large bowl, stir together oats, salt, cinnamon and nutmeg. Add the maple syrup and oil, mixing well. Add pistachios, flaxseeds, pumpkin seeds and sunflower seeds. Stir to combine thoroughly.

Spread mixture on a large baking sheet in a thin layer. Bake for 30 to 40 minutes or until granola is crisp, stirring once or twice to brown evenly. Remove from oven and cool slightly. Mix in cranberries and apricots. When completely cool, transfer to an airtight container. Keeps for up to two weeks.

· THE LOCAL GROCER ·

Suzanne Bergeron

When their daughters were little, Suzanne Bergeron and Antonio Drouin would load up the car and head off on long, meandering Quebec vacations, building sandcastles on the beach in Gaspé, visiting farms in the Charlevoix hills. They would sample homemade berry jams, smoked fish and tomato chutney from farm stands and village stores. Back home in Montreal, though, all that delicious, down-home Quebec fare was hard to find. "In the supermarket, we had at our feet mangoes and coconuts, kiwis and curry sauces – the most exotic foods from the farthest corners of the world," Bergeron recalls. "Everything except our own."

So she and Drouin hatched a plan to reconnect Montrealers with their *terroir*. In 2000, they opened Le Marché des Saveurs, the grocery store they run with the help of their daughters, Isabelle and Julie, and their son-in-law Simon. The store is a throwback to another time. Every single item here was grown, raised, preserved or transformed within Quebec's borders. Homemade preserves, apple cider vinegars and dozens of honeys, syrups, cheeses, compotes and tisanes are delivered by the jam makers, beekeepers and brewers themselves. A whole section of the store is devoted to Quebec wines, liqueurs and ciders. In the refrigerators, there is rabbit terrine from Stanstead, duck confit from St-Ferréol-les-Neiges, and butter hand-churned every day on a farm in Compton with 60 cows. There is artisanal beer from Mont-Laurier and frozen moussaka baked and blessed by an order of Greek Orthodox nuns in the kitchen of their monastery, nestled in the woods north of Lachute. In late summer, after Christian Champy has harvested his sunflowers in Upton, there will be a shipment of golden sunflower oil.

"Our customers don't want to do groceries with a dictionary, trying to decipher the ingredients on the label," Bergeron says. "They want food that is basic, real and traceable. And local. They want to know who made it, where and how. They want food with a story."

Suzanne au marché

Appletini

A splash of sweet Quebec ice cider blunts the impact of the classic vodka martini.

3 oz (90 ml) vodka
1 oz (30 ml) ice cider
apple slice, for garnish

In a cocktail shaker filled with ice, shake vodka and ice cider. Strain into a chilled martini glass. Garnish with a thin slice of apple.

A Twist of Quebec

Eating isn't all there is to the local food movement. Quebec has a long, proud tradition of beer, liqueur and cider-making. Raise a glass to the 100-mile diet with a cocktail that evokes a Laurentian forest or an Eastern Townships maple grove by incorporating quintessentially Quebec ingredients like cranberry, maple syrup, ice cider and spruce beer.

Spruce Beer Mojito

Spruce beer is thoroughly Québécois. Its evergreen notes give this Cuban classic a decidedly winter feel.

1 handful fresh mint leaves
1 tsp sugar
1½ oz (45 ml) white rum
juice of ½ lime
4 oz (125 ml) spruce beer
2 oz (60 ml) cranberry juice

Place mint leaves in a tall highball glass. Muddle with sugar, rum and lime juice. Top up with spruce beer and cranberry juice. Add ice.

Le Jean Talon

A local version of the famous kir royale featuring sparkling cider from Rougemont and cassis from Île d'Orléans.

3 oz (90 ml) sparkling cider
½ oz (15 ml) cassis

Combine the sparkling cider and cassis in a tall champagne flute. If desired, garnish with a bamboo skewer studded with fresh cranberries.

· THE WINTER CAMPER ·

Lionel Filion

It's Christmas Eve and shoppers hurry from stall to stall for last-minute provisions. Outside, children chase each other through the maze of trees, carpeting the snow-packed ground in needles. Lionel Filion, a lumberjack of a man with a booming voice, massive hands and twinkling eyes, emerges from the warmth of his camper trailer and pulls his toque over his ears. In the month since they set up camp at the market, the Filion family has sold more than 3,500 balsam firs, spruces and white pines, now twinkling and shimmering in living rooms across the city. They have taken turns sleeping in the trailer in teams of two, watching over their trees, subsisting on fast food and peanut butter sandwiches, darting into the market early in the morning to use the showers at the back of the building.

For more than three decades, the Filions have been coming to the market to sell Christmas trees grown on the family farm in the Eastern Townships. "My father and my grandfather before him spent their lives in the woods, with an axe in their hands," Filion says. He grew up one of eight children in a poor family and his earliest Christmas memories are of plates of food brought to the door by charitable neighbours. As if to return the favour, Filion turns the parking lot at Jean Talon Market into a winter wonderland every December. He installs lampposts, strings them with coloured lights and hangs ribboned wreaths and garlands all around. Sitting at the table in his trailer, warming up a spell, tears well in Filion's eyes as he remembers a trio of little girls who turned up at the market one Christmas Eve long ago. "Sir, can we sing you a carol in exchange for a Christmas tree?" they pleaded.

A few years ago, a well-dressed woman turned up to buy her Christmas tree. "You probably don't remember me," she told Filion. "Many, many Christmases ago, my sisters and I sang for you and you gave us a tree." Their father had just walked out on the family. Their mother had no money. That tree was all the holiday they had that year. "I've been wanting to thank you for that," she said.

It is not yet 3 p.m., but already the December sky is darkening. Only a few last-minute stragglers turn up. Filion's grandson is throwing the last of the unsold trees into the back of the truck. Soon they will pull up stakes and head home to Ayer's Cliff, cold and tired, ready for their own Christmas celebrations. Already, Filion can taste the tourtière.

Lionel, Les Sapins Filion

"Winter arrived in the middle of the night, a few tentative flakes building to a steady tumble. By morning Montreal is blanketed in snow.

A little boy shovels the entrance to his father's fruit store, pushing the heavy snow with all his might, stopping to catch a fat, white snowflake on his tongue. Someone has built a miniature snowman on the bench outside Marché des Saveurs. His arms are twigs and he has black olives for eyes."

PAIX ET AMOUR

Granita à l'Épinette

Spruce beer-flavoured granita looks like freshly fallen snow and smells and tastes of a boreal forest. Spruce beer, best known as *bière d'épinette*, is an old-time Quebec classic, sold in just about every supermarket and dépanneur. It's a non-alcoholic soft drink flavoured with the buds, needles or essence of spruce.

Serve this frozen treat in tiny porcelain bowls, or in stemmed liqueur glasses with a shot of Calvados or frozen vodka. It's a refreshing dessert or a palate cleanser between courses – what we call a *trou Normand*.

(Serves 6)

2 cups (500 ml) spruce beer
½ cup (125 ml) sugar
6 juniper berries
juice and finely grated zest of 1 large lemon

In a saucepan over medium heat, combine spruce beer and sugar and heat, stirring, until sugar dissolves. Add juniper berries and crush with the end of a wooden spoon. Continue simmering over low heat for 5 minutes. Remove from heat and strain through a sieve into a shallow glass pan. Add lemon juice and zest and stir.

Freeze until granita is firm, at least 2 hours. To serve, scrape the ice's surface with a fork, then spoon the shavings into serving bowls or glasses. Garnish with sprigs of spruce or juniper.

Léopoldo
Fruits & Légumes
SERVICE DE RESTAURATION

514-273-5456

Index & recipes

Index & ingredients

Index & portraits

ACKNOWLEDGEMENTS

This book has been more than a year and a half in the making, an odyssey that has taken me into Jean Talon Market's every nook and cranny, and across Quebec chasing the best of the seasons in all kinds of weather.

None of it would have been possible without the generosity of the market's farmers, food crafters and vendors, the tireless men and women who are the heart and soul of Marché Jean-Talon. They shared their passion and their food and recipes, invited me behind the counter and then back to the farm, greeting my endless questions with patience and kindness. Over lunch or dinner, or during a short break leaning against a tractor in the field or sorting peppers behind the stall, they shared the stories and recipes that are this book's treasures. I thank all of them from the bottom of my heart, especially **Jacques Rémillard**, for his generosity and unflagging enthusiasm; **Liette Lauzon**, who took me under her wing; **Tony Passarelli**, a horticultural encyclopedia, who introduced me to a lettuce called Lola and taught me to pickle peppers and plant a fig tree; his colleagues at the **Birri Brothers** stall for always making me feel at home under the big burgundy canopy; and to to **James Henry** & **Charles Atkins** and **Christian Servant** for their open-hearted Gaspesian hospitality. Thanks also to **Marc Angers**, Isabelle Letourneau and **Benoit Gagnon** for their behind-the-scenes assistance at the market, and to **Stéphane Ricci** for his vision of what makes a market great.

I am ever grateful to my husband and Saturday-morning market partner, **Daniel Mainardi**, who has always believed in me, and my daughter **Katherine** and my son **Alexander**. They have all given so much – taste-testing recipes, grilling kebabs, washing dishes, sharpening knives, peeling and chopping mountains of apples, squash and beets. They grace my table – and my life – with warmth, laughter and love.

My gratitude to **Albert Elbilia**, photographer, designer and kindred spirit, for the unique way he harnesses light and sees the world; for his brilliant photographs and stunning layouts; and especially for his enthusiasm and boundless sense of fun. Many thanks to **Stéphane Losq**, production manager, navigator, diplomat, sommelier, sherpa guide and troubleshooter extraordinaire. Thank you to **Sheila Scott**, every writer's dream editor with her eagle-eyed attention to detail and deft and gentle handling of the prose. And to translator **Joelle Bernier**, who took my English text and fashioned it so eloquently into the French edition of this book. Thanks to **Vanessa Tobin** and **Katherine Mainardi** for their smooth, seamless assistance in the kitchen during photo shoots; and to **Alexander Mainardi** for technical support. I also wish to express heartfelt gratitude to my publishers at **Les Éditions Cardinal**. To **Richard Trempe**, who listened to my market tales and heard in them the makings of a beautiful book; and to **Antoine Ross Trempe**, for his trust and the artistic freedom he allowed me.

And to all those who have been a part of the making of this book in one way or another, **thank you**: To Silvija Ulmanis, Jan Gregory, Margaret Stewart, Joanne Semenak, Richard Mainardi, Orysia Krywiak, and Renée Fournier at Arthur Quentin and Guillaume De L'Isle at L'Emouleur, for sharing plates, platters and knives. For friendship and creative genius, thanks to **Peggy Curran**, **Donna Nebenzahl**, **Susan Schwartz** and **Catherine Wallace**, who listened to the first tales and read the final versions.

To Maria Loggia for culinary inspiration and stellar alignment; **James Mennie** for historical and moral support; **Jane Pavanel** for all kinds of advice; **Louise Rousseau** and **Alain Prud'homme** for maple mousse and restaurant ramblings; **Lois Cianflone** who inspired the cauliflower fusilli; **Johanne Martineau** for her calming influence; and **Stéphanie Gaudet** for fish cakes and iced coffee in Hochelaga-Maisonneuve during the home stretch. To **Jenny May Trudeau** for Spanish to English translation; to **Lorraine Lebel** for the Moroccan cooking class; to **Dinu Bumbaru** of **Heritage Montreal**; Isabelle St-Germain of **Equiterre**; André Plante of the **Quebec Market Growers Association**; **Elena Faita** of **Quincaillerie Dante**; and to **Paul-Louis Martin**, author of **Les Fruits du Québec** for the story of the Mont Royal plum's birth.

And to my **Mom**, who taught me to cook and always cleaned up the mess.

Susan Semenak is a Montreal journalist, food writer and artist. Her stories, recipes and food styling appear regularly in Montreal's The Gazette. Her work has also been published in the National Post, Maclean's magazine and the International Herald Tribune.

Semenak's cooking, writing and art are all shaped by the moods and rhythms of Montreal, her native city.